D1260282

AT THE SHRINE OF
ST. CHARLES

THE CHARLES LAMB MEMORIAL FOUNTAIN
By Margaret Wrightson
In the Garden of the Inner Temple

AT THE SHRINE OF
ST. CHARLES

STRAY PAPERS ON LAMB
BROUGHT TOGETHER FOR THE
CENTENARY OF HIS DEATH IN
1834

BY

E. V. LUCAS
AUTHOR OF "TURNING THINGS OVER"
"A ROVER I WOULD BE: ESSAYS AND FANTASIES," ETC.

WITH A SPECIAL PREFACE
FOR THE AMERICAN EDITION

FOUR ILLUSTRATIONS

NEW YORK
E. P. DUTTON & CO., INC.
PUBLISHERS

PRINTED IN THE UNITED STATES OF AMERICA
BY THE POLYGRAPHIC COMPANY OF AMERICA, N.Y.

TO

THOMAS J. WISE

BEST AND MOST GENEROUS

OF BOOK-COLLECTORS

PREFACE TO THE AMERICAN EDITION

IT is never time to send a book to the press; or, in other words, we live and learn. When this book was published in London, in February, 1934, I was unaware of certain things which a month later I learned during a visit to America, spent principally among the collections of Eliana which, although Lamb once defiantly declared that he would henceforth write "for antiquity," abound in that country. For instance, I had to come to America to learn that Lamb's cousin, the bookbinder, had been discovered by the late Major Butterworth to have been named Lovekin. To me, an even more interesting fact imparted by one of the most patient and thorough of students of our author's writings, Mr. Ralph C. Beals, is that a letter preserved in America, to Charles Ollier of the *New Monthly Magazine,* states definitely that Mrs. Conrady was a fictitious creation both in name and appearance, thus making one of the essays in this book practically negligible. I have left it in for the sake of the quotations from Lamb that adorn it; but its questions are answered. I may also add that a movement is now afoot in England to erect during the current year a memorial to Lamb in the little garden (once the burial ground) of Christ Church, off Newgate Street, which Lamb as a Blue Coat boy passed by, on his way to service, every day for seven years.

E. V. L.

New York
April 9, 1934

CONTENTS

ILLUSTRATIONS

'LAMB's postscript [to the letter to Bernard Barton of December 1, 1824] is written in extremely small characters, and the letters of the two lines of verse are in alternate red and black inks. It was this letter which, Edward FitzGerald tells us, Thackeray pressed to his forehead, with the remark "Saint Charles!" Hitherto, the postscript not having been thought worthy of print by previous editors, it was a little difficult to understand why this particular letter had been selected for Thackeray's epithet. But when one thinks of the patience with which, after making gentle fun of her father, Lamb sat down to amuse Lucy Barton, and, with Thackeray, thinks also of his whole life, it becomes more clear.'

From *The Works of Charles and Mary Lamb*, Letters, Vol. vi.

Edited by E. V. LUCAS

HIS COUSIN THE BOOKBINDER

'Oh, I am so poorly! I waked it at my cousin's, the bookbinder, who is now with God.'—*Charles Lamb to P. G. Patmore*, 1827

'SO you've been reading *Elia's* essays, sir, have you? I have a copy too. I'll fetch it and show you. . . . The inscription? Oh yes, that's all right. He's my cousin, true enough: his real name's not Elia, of course; his real name's Lamb—Charles Lamb. He's a clerk at the East India Company's in Leadenhall Street—a little dark man with a large head. Must be nearly fifty by this time.

' "Genius", you say? Well, I've heard others say that too—one or two persons, that is: customers of mine; but I don't know. Perhaps I'm no judge of such things, I'm a bookbinder. The outside of books is my line, not the inside. Besides, he's a relation of mine.

' "Genius", you say? My idea of genius is not that. I like a straightforward thing. Did you ever read the *Elegy in a Country Churchyard*, by Thomas Gray? Now, there's genius. So beautifully it goes—never a trip in the tongue from beginning to end, and everything so clear a child could understand it, and yet it's literature too. My little girl used to speak it. *Rasselas*, too—do you know that? The Happy Valley and all the rest of it. That's genius, I think. But not this twisted stuff going backwards and forwards, and one never feeling quite sure how to take it. I like a clever man with a plain mind.

'It's just the same with my cousin when you meet him. You never know what he's at. He's so nice sometimes, all heart, and friendly—and then the next time I have a notion that everything he says means something else. He leads me on to talk—just as I am talking now to you, sir,—and he seems to agree so warmly with what I say; and then all of a sudden I see that he's just making fun of me all the time. He must have his joke. He comes in here sometimes on his way from the office; and precious little he does there, I can tell you. Oh, they're an easy lot, those East India clerks.

'But with all his odd ways and that mischievous mouth of his, his heart's in the right place. Very different from his brother, who died a year or so back. He was nothing to boast of; but the airs that man used to put on! I remember his father well—a little brisk man, wonderfully like Garrick, full of jokes and bright, quick ways. He was really a scrivener, but he didn't do much of that in those days, having fallen into an easy place with old Mr. Salt, the Member of Parliament and a great man in the law. This Mr. Salt lived in the Temple, and little John Lamb—that is your Elia's father—he was his servant: did everything for him and lived in clover. Mrs. Lamb, she cooked. Mr. Salt was the generous kind—sent the boys to school and all the rest of it. They had it their own way till the old gentleman died, and then things went wrong one after the other. It's too sad to talk about. . . .

'Except that Mrs. Lamb and her husband's sister, Miss Sarah—"Aunt Hetty" they used to call her—never quite hit it off, it was as happy a family as you'd ask for. But there came terrible times. . . . It's too sad. Where was I?—Oh yes, so you see that Mr. John Lamb, Esquire, who died the other day, had little enough to boast of, but he walked about as if he owned the earth. He used to come in here now and then to give me an order, and he threw it to me as if it was a bone to a dog. Many's the time I had it on my tongue to remind him what his father was, but I kept it back. A word unsaid is still to say. He was at the South Sea House, near his brother in Leadenhall Street, but they didn't have much to do with each other. My Lord John, he was a big, blustering, prosperous man, while this little one who calls himself Elia is all for quietness and not being seen, and having his own thoughts and his own jokes. They hadn't much in common. . . .

'Besides, there was another thing. There's a sister, you must know, sir, a wonderful wise woman, but she's not always quite right in her head, poor dear; and when it was a question of whether someone had to promise to be responsible for her, or she must go to an asylum for the rest of her life, her younger brother, the writer of that book there, under your arm, said he would; and he gave up everything, and has taken care of her—it was thirty years ago very nearly—ever since. Well, it was thought in the family and by their friends that John, who was a grown man at the time and a bachelor then (he married a widow later and I hope had to pay for it), and was beginning to be well to do, ought to have

done more than he did; and I think that
sometimes he thought so too, although he was
usually pretty well satisfied with himself. Anyway, he didn't go to see his brother and sister
much, and when he did I've heard there was
often trouble, because he would have his own
way and argufy until he lost his temper. I was
told as how he once had a dispute with Mr.
Hazlitt, the writer, over something to do with
pictures, and knocked him down. Just think
of knocking a man down about a matter of
paint! But there's some high-handed men that
would quarrel over anything.

'Like his little brother, he tried writing too,
but he couldn't do it. He wrote a little tract
on kindness to animals, and brought it here to
be bound in morocco. Not to give away, mind,
but to keep. "Author's Copy" I had to letter
it. . . . "Kindness to animals," I nearly said
to him; "what about kindness to sisters?" But
I didn't say it.

'The sister? Ah yes, she's the pick. She's a
great woman, if ever there was one. I know
her better than any of them, because when they
were living near here, and her brother—your
Mr. Lamb, the author—was at his office, I
often looked in with a pork chop or some little
thing like that. There's no jokes about her, no

5

saying things that she doesn't mean, or anything like that. She's all gold, my cousin Mary
is. She understands everything, too. I've taken
lots of troubles to her—little difficulties about
my children, and what not—and she understands directly, for all she's an old maid, and
tells me just what I want to know. She's the
clever one. She can write, too. I've got a little
book of her stories and some poetry for children
—here they are—I bound them myself: that's
the best binding I can do—real russia, and
hand tooling, every bit of it. Did she write all
of them? No, she didn't write all, but she
wrote the best. Her brother Charles did something to each, but I don't mind that. I think
of them as her books—Mary's. If only she had
better health, she would write much better
than he does; but her poor head. . . . Every
year, you must know, she goes out of her mind
for a little while and has to be put away. Oh,
it's too sad. . . . It makes me ashamed of
being what you scholarly gentlemen call
compos mentis.

'Have they many friends? Oh yes, a good
many. Most of them are too clever for me; but
there are some old-fashioned ones too, that
they like for old sakes' sake. They're the best.
One or two of them are very good customers

6

of mine. There's Mr. Crabb Robinson, the barrister, he brings me lots of books to mend, and I've had work for Mr. Aders, too. But as for your Mr. Lamb,—Elia,—never a stitch will he let you put into any book, even if it's dropping to pieces. Why, he won't even take the dealer's tickets off them. He never thinks of the outside of a book, but you should see him tearing the heart out of them by the light of one candle. I'm told he knows more about what books are worth reading than anyone living. That's odd, isn't it, and his father a little serving-man! Life's full of surprises. They say he knows all about poetry, too, and helped the great poets. There's Mr. Wordsworth, why, he dedicated a book to my cousin,—I've got it here, *The Waggoner*, a pretty book it is, too,— and Mr. Coleridge, who wrote about the old sailor man and the albatross, he let my cousin put some little poems of his own into one of his books. It turns one inside out when one thinks of this, and then of the old days and his father powdering Mr. Salt's wig. But I suppose everyone's father had to work once. Still, it's funnier when one belongs to the same family.

'Now I come to remember it, his father used to write a little too—free and easy pieces for a charitable society he belonged to, and so on.

But there won't be any more Lambs to write—
John left no children, only a stepdaughter,
and Charles and Mary are single. And the
less said about the brains of my lot the better.
This is the end. Well . . .

'Yes, they've moved from London now.
They're living in Islington. They used to live
in the Temple, for years, and then they went
to Covent Garden, over a tinman's. Miss Lamb
liked that better than the Temple, but her
brother liked the Temple best. It gave her
more to do, poor dear, during the day, because
her sitting-room window looked over Bow
Street, and she could see all that was going on
and the runners bringing in the scamps and
thieves. I'm afraid Islington is very dull after
that. She was close to the two great theatres,
too, and they both love the play.

'He wrote a farce once. I went to see it.
Nearly twenty years ago, at the Lane, when
Elliston had it. We had orders for the pit, my
wife and I, and the house was full of clerks
from the South Sea House and the East India
House. But it wouldn't do. *Mr. H.* it was called,
and the whole joke was about the man's full
name. But it wouldn't do. No one really minds
names, and his wasn't so monstrously bad—
only Hogsflesh when all was said and done.

8

All of us did what we could for it, and the gentlemen from the great offices cheered and clapped, but the Noes got it. I never heard such hissing. I climbed up on the seat to see how poor Miss Lamb and her brother were taking it,—they were right in front, just by the orchestra,—and there was he, hissing away louder than anyone. Think of it, hissing his own play! It's one of the best jokes I ever heard. But she, poor dear, she was crying.

'I went up to Islington to see them, only last week, but he was out. A nice little cottage, but very quiet for her. Nothing to see but the houses over the way, and the New River, and the boys fishing for sticklebacks all day long. The river's absolutely in front of the house: nothing between you and it. Have you ever heard of Mr. Dyer, the writer? An old man, nearly blind. Well, he was coming away from my cousin's one day last year, and he walked bang into the water before anyone could stop him. Plump in. It's a wonder he wasn't drowned. There was an account of it in the *London Magazine* for December; for my cousin's a terrible man to serve up his friends and have jokes against them. He writes about everything just as it happens. I'm always expecting he'll have me in one of his essays. In fact, to tell you a secret, sir, that's why I read them—to find out. But I don't think he's had me yet.

'Yes, Islington's very different from Covent Garden, and the Temple too; for though the Temple is quiet enough, you've only got to pop into Fleet Street to be in the thick of everything. When they lived there Mary used to like doing her shopping in Fetter Lane, because it was at the top of the lane that she used to go to school years and years ago. For she's getting to be an old woman, you know. Let me see, how old is she? Why, let's see, when was Mary born? It must have been 1763; no, it was 1764. Bless my soul, she'll be sixty this year.

'What does she do all day? Well, she reads a great deal, stories for the most part. And she sews. She's very good with her needle. And then she has her thoughts. And at night they play cards. He gets back pretty soon, you know. Those East India gentlemen, they don't do too much, I can tell you, and I'm told he's one of the laziest. Always either joking or writing letters, I hear. There's a good story of him down there. One of the superiors met him coming in at about half-past ten, and he said to him, sharp-like, "Mr. Lamb," he said, "you come very late." And what do you think my

cousin said, the impudent little fellow? "Yes,"
he said, as cool as you like, "yes," he said,
"but see how early I go." I can't say it as he
did, because he stammers and stutters and I'm
no mimic : but the brass of it shut the gentleman
up. My cousin told me himself. He likes to tell
you his good things ; but I can't understand a
lot of them. Everyone has a different idea of
what's funny. I'm with him, though, about old
Munden : I could laugh at him all night.

'I'm troubled about them up there, so far
from London and the theatres and the noise.
It's a mistake to give up so much all at once.
And they've given up their regular evenings,
too, when people came in to play cards and
talk. You can't ask busy folk to go to Islington.

'My cousin told me some bad news last week.
She says that your Mr. Lamb,—Elia,—although
he has such an easy time and a decent salary,
wants to leave the East India House and do
nothing. I hope they won't let him. I know
enough of life and of him to see what a mistake
it would be. It was a mistake to go to Islington :
it will be a worse mistake to retire. He says he
wants to live in the country; but he doesn't
really. Authors don't know what they want.
I always say that every author ought to have a
bookbinder to advise him. Yes, sir, or a sister.

'She knows it's all wrong, poor dear, but what can she do? He worries so. She sees him all miserable, and after she's said all she can against his plans, she agrees with them. That's like good women. When they see that what must be must be, they stop. But it is very sad. . . . It's her I'm so sorry for. He's the kind of man that ought to go to business every day.

'Well, sir, good night to you. I hope I haven't been tedious with all my talk.

'No, sir, not a genius; but very clever, I grant you.'

1907

RANDAL NORRIS
The Last to Call him Charley
1751–1827
From the Miniature by Matilda Betham
By permission of Mr. C. W. B. Richardson

THE LAST TO CALL HIM CHARLEY

FORTUNATE circumstances having just put me in possession of a photograph of the miniature portrait of Lamb's friend Randal Norris (the last to call him Charley), I am eager that others should see it too, for there can be no member of that vanished circle in and about the Temple who is nearer our hearts than the kindly 'R. N.' of the essay entitled 'A Death-Bed' in the first edition of the second *Elia* volume. Hence the reproduction in this book.

Our first definite glimpse of Randal Norris, who was Sub-Treasurer and Librarian of the Inner Temple for many years before his death in 1827, is in the postscript to the essay on 'The Old Benchers of the Inner Temple', written in 1821, where Lamb says that he went to him —to R. N.—for information about Samuel Salt, who, it will be remembered, was the employer of Lamb's father. But it is more than probable— in fact, I think, certain—that the 'Mr. Norris of Christ's Hospital' who, after the tragedy in the Lamb household in 1796, was, in Lamb's words, 'as a father to me', was this same worthy man.

In 1796 he was forty-five, having been born in 1751, and we know that he had known Lamb from childhood, for in 'A Death-Bed' it is so stated: 'he was my friend and my father's friend for all the life that I can remember. . . . He was the last link that bound me to the Temple.' I have not been able to trace Randal Norris to Christ's Hospital, but, when fortified by Lamb's remark about Norris in a letter to Wordsworth in 1830—he was 'sixty years ours and our father's friend'—it is reasonable enough to assume that he may have had an official post there before he went to serve the perusing lawyers.

The passage in the piteous letter of 1796 continues: 'Mrs. Norris as a mother; though we had few claims on them.' But as for 'claims', it would be enough for the Norrises that Mrs. Norris had been brought up at Widford and knew there Lamb's maternal grandmother, Mrs. Field.

I have referred to 'A Death-Bed', but since that was but a reproduction, with the names altered, of the famous and beautiful letter to Crabb Robinson on January 20, 1827, let me refresh memories by quoting the letter rather than the essay:

DEAR ROBINSON,

    I called upon you this morning, and found that you were gone to visit a dying friend. I had been upon a like errand. Poor Norris has been lying dying for now almost a week, such is the penalty we pay for having enjoyed a strong constitution! Whether he knew me or not, I know not, or whether he saw me through his poor glazed eyes; but the group I saw about him I shall not forget. Upon the bed, or about it, were assembled his wife and two daughters, and poor deaf Richard, his son, looking doubly stupefied. There they were, and seemed to have been sitting all the week. I could only reach out a hand to Mrs. Norris. Speaking was impossible in that mute chamber. By this time I hope it is all over with him.

    In him I have a loss the world cannot make up. He was my friend and my father's friend all the life I can remember. I seem to have made foolish friendships ever since. Those are friendships which outlive a second generation. Old as I am waxing, in his eyes I was still the child he first knew me.[1] To the last he called me Charley. I have none to call me Charley now. He was the last link that bound me to the Temple. You are but of yesterday. In him seem to have died the old plainness of manners and singleness of heart. Letters he knew nothing of, nor did his reading extend beyond the pages of the *Gentleman's Magazine*. Yet there was a pride of literature

---

[1] Lamb was then nearing fifty-two.

about him from being amongst books (he was
librarian), and from some scraps of doubtful
Latin which he had picked up in his office of
entering students, that gave him very diverting
airs of pedantry. Can I forget the erudite look
with which, when he had been in vain trying to
make out a black-letter text of Chaucer in the
Temple Library, he laid it down and told me that
—'in those old books, Charley, there is sometimes
a deal of indifferent spelling'; and seemed to
console himself in the reflection!

His jokes, for he had his jokes, are now ended,
but they were old trusty perennials, staples
that pleased after *decies repetita*, and were always
as good as new. One song he had, which was
reserved for the night of Christmas-day, which
we always spent in the Temple. It was an old
thing, and spoke of the flat bottoms of our foes
and the possibility of their coming over in dark-
ness, and alluded to threats of an invasion many
years blown over; and when he came to the part

We'll still make 'em run, and we'll still make 'em sweat,
In spite of the devil and *Brussels Gazette*!

his eyes would sparkle as with the freshness of an
impending event. And what is the *Brussels
Gazette* now? I cry while I enumerate these
trifles. 'How shall we tell them in a stranger's
ear?'

His poor good girls will now have to receive
their afflicted mother in an inaccessible hovel in
an obscure village in Herts, where they have been
long struggling to make a school without effect;

and poor deaf Richard—and the more helpless for being so—is thrown on the wide world.

My first motive in writing, and, indeed, in calling on you, was to ask if you were enough acquainted with any of the Benchers, to lay a plain statement before them of the circumstances of the family. I almost fear not, for you are of another hall. But if you can oblige me and my poor friend, who is now insensible to any favours, pray exert yourself. You cannot say too much good of poor Norris and his poor wife.

Yours ever,

CHARLES LAMB

Later, Lamb thought it better to approach members of Norris's own hall and, in the end, a pension of £80 was secured for the widow.

Of Randal Norris we know only what Lamb tells us. But there lately have come to me, through the courtesy of Mrs. Julia Towndrow of Kettering, a descendant, two letters in his own hand, and as both contain the latest tidings of Mr. and Miss Lamb up to the moment of writing—stop press news, in short— they have an interest far beyond that of their staple subject-matter. For to read in the faded ink of more than a century ago what Mr. and Miss Lamb were doing is to bring the Brother and Sister very near to us. The first, dated Inner Temple, August 6, 1823, is to the Misses

Norris at Widford, Herts, wishing them well with their school and urging them not to despair if success does not come at once. 'Tell your Mother that the Lambs have taken a House in Colebrook Row, Islington, have left Russell Street and will leave Dalston very soon where Mary is and Miss James. She has been ill but is recovering. Mr. Lamb thinks it was occasioned by [merely] thinking of the removal, for she had no trouble in it.'

Miss James was Mary Lamb's devoted nurse for many years: indeed, till her death, as we shall see. 'Give my Love to your Mother,' the writer also says, 'and tell her Richard and Self are quite well and do not wish her to come home sooner on our account, as we jog on very well.'

The next letter, dated September 28, 1825, is to Mrs. Norris, who was again staying at Widford, and it is chiefly about some building alterations to a house there. 'Dear Betsy,' it begins, and the last sentence runs, 'I am sorry to say I have just heard by Miss Emma that Mr. and Miss Lamb are both unwell and the more so as it is Miss Lamb's old complaint she is afflicted with, Charles having wrote to Miss Emma not to come to the House as is usual at Michaelmas.' Emma, of course, was Emma

Isola, the Lambs' adopted child, then away teaching.

Randal Norris died in 1827 and was buried in the Temple, and we come now to the survivors—Mrs. Norris, the two daughters Elizabeth and Jane, and the deaf son Richard, all henceforward to be living at Widford. With the Misses Norris and Richard I chanced, at a single remove, to come, in 1902, in touch, when I was preparing a biography of Lamb, for through my friend the late W. J. Craig, the Shakespearean scholar and philologist and an adorer of Elia, I had an introduction to Mrs. Elizabeth Coe, a very old but sprightly lady living at Berkhampsted, who as a child had been a pupil of the Misses Norris and remembered Lamb's visits; and Craig and I went down together one afternoon to have tea with her and to collect her reminiscences. Subsequently I wrote for the *Athenaeum* the following account of our experiences, extracts from which were afterwards incorporated in my book:

We have very little knowledge of Lamb's ways with children; but enough to show that he must have been very good company with them when he liked. He cannot have been thrown much among them. There is his charming letter to his 'child-wife', Sophy Kenney, and the allusion, in the same vein, to little Louisa Martin (whom he called Monkey), in the letter to Hazlitt of November 10, 1805:

'Some things too about Monkey which can't so well be written: how it set up for a fine lady, and thought it had got lovers, and was obliged to be convinced of its age from the parish register, where it was proved to be only twelve; and an edict issued, that it should not give itself airs yet these four years; and how it got leave to be called Miss, by grace.'

And in an unpublished letter from Mary Lamb to Dorothy Wordsworth I read that John Hazlitt's little girl was so fond of Charles Lamb that, when he was expected, she used to stop strangers in the street and tell them 'Mr. Lamb is coming to-night'.

There is also a passage in Charles and Mary Cowden Clarke's *Recollections of Writers* which is so much of a piece with Mrs. Coe's reminiscences that I copy it here:

'Charles Lamb brought a choice condiment in the shape of a jar of preserved ginger for the little Novellos' delectation; and when some officious elder suggested that it was lost upon children, and therefore had better be reserved for the grown-up people, Lamb would not hear of the transfer, but insisted that children were excellent judges of good things, and that they must and should have the cate in question. He was right, for long did the remembrance remain in the family of that delicious rarity, and of the mode in which "Mr. Lamb" stalked up and down the passage with a mysterious harbingering look and stride, muttering something that sounded like a conjuration, holding the precious jar under his arm, and feigning to have found it stowed away in a dark chimney somewhere near.'

Beyond these references, and a few others, there is little evidence as to Lamb's attitude to children, for whom he wrote so much.

Mrs. Coe, in her eighty-fourth year, remembers Lamb as he was between 1827 and 1833. In 1827 —aged fifty-two and free of the India House— he used often to walk down to Widford—twenty-two miles from London—to stay a day or two among old friends and older associations. These little visits probably signified that Mary Lamb was ill, for Mrs. Coe does not remember that Mary Lamb ever accompanied her brother. At any rate, she never saw her. Miss Isola, she says, came with him once, and her feet were so sore from the journey that she had to lie in bed for two or three days, Mr. Lamb waiting for her recovery. Mr. Lamb often had blisters too, but he did not seem to mind. He loved walking too much.

Lamb's chief friends at Widford in those days were the Norrises. The sisters were known as Miss Betsy and Miss Jane. Mrs. Norris was the good angel of the village: doctor, nurse, and every one's refuge in trouble. Mr. Richard Norris, who was deaf and peculiar, lived in the house too.

Among the pupils at Goddard House was Elizabeth Hunt, one of the three little daughters of Thomas Hunt, of the Widford water-mill, whose wife and Mrs. Norris were old friends.

In those days—seventy and more years ago—she was Mr. Lamb's favourite of all the Widford children—partly, she suspects, from her quickness in catching a mischievous idea. She remembers, with a vividness that is, to some extent, communicable, his affected conviction that her hair curled only by artificial means, and his repeated warnings at bedtime that she must on no account forget to put in her papers. 'But I don't have to curl it, Mr. Lamb, I don't, I don't.' 'Well, bring me a mug of beer from old Bogey and we'll say no more about it.' Old Bogey was the big cask. For, as a rule, when Mr. Lamb walked down to see the Norrises, he used to sleep at the mill. 'Now, Mrs. Hunt,' he would say, 'are you going to let me creep into a goose's belly to-night?' for he always had his joke, and no one would expect him to call a feather-bed a 'feather-bed', like other folks. He said it was like heaven, in a goose's belly. When he made a joke he did not laugh himself.

He always brought a book with him, sometimes several, and he would read or write a great deal. His clothes were rusty and shabby, like a poor Dissenting minister's. He was very thin and looked half-starved, partly the effect of high cheek-bones. He wore knee-breeches and gaiters and a high stock. He carried a walking-stick with which he used to strike at pebbles. He smoked a black clay pipe. No one would have taken him for what he was, but he was clearly a man apart. He took pleasure in looking eccentric. He was proud of being *the* Mr. Lamb.

Mrs. Coe does not remember anything about Mr. Lamb's taste in food, except that he was fond of turnips. He used to come down to breakfast late.

He was very free with his money. To beggars he always gave: just what his hand happened to draw from his pocket, even as much as three shillings. 'Poor devil! he wants it more than I do; and I've got plenty,' he used to say. He would take the children into the village to the little general shop. It had a door cut in two, like a butcher's, and he would lean over the lower half and rap his stick on the floor, calling loudly, 'Abigail Ives! Abigail Ives!' 'Ah, Mr. Lamb,' she used to reply from the inner room, 'I thought I knew your rap.' 'Yes, Abigail, it is I,' he would say, 'and I've got my money with me. Give these young ladies sixpennyworth of Gibraltar rock.' Gibraltar rock was Abigail Ives's speciality, and sixpennyworth was an unheard-of amount except when Mr. Lamb was in the village. It had to be broken with a hammer. The children, Mrs. Coe says, always stood a little in awe of his unlikeness to other people, in spite of these treats.

When he joined the Norrises' dinner-table he kept every one laughing. Mr. Richard sat at one end, and some of the school children would be there too. One day Mr. Lamb gave every one a fancy name all round the table, and made a verse on each. 'You are so-and-so,' he said, 'and you are so-and-so,' adding the rhyme. 'What's he

23

saying? What are you laughing at?' Mr. Richard asked testily, for he was short-tempered. Miss Betsy explained the joke to him, and Mr. Lamb, coming to his turn, said—only he said it in verse —'Now, Dick, it's your turn. I shall call you Gruborum; because all you think of is your food and your stomach.' Mr. Richard pushed back his chair in a rage and stamped out of the room. 'Now I've done it,' said Mr. Lamb, 'I must go and make friends with my old chum. Give me a large plate of pudding to take to him.' When he came back he said, 'It's all right. I thought the pudding would do it.' Mr. Lamb and Mr. Richard never got on very well, and Mr. Richard didn't like his teasing ways at all; but Mr. Lamb often went for long walks with him, because no one else would. He did many kind things like that.

There used to be a half-holiday when Mr. Lamb came, partly because he would force his way into the schoolroom and make seriousness impossible. His head would suddenly appear at the door in the midst of lessons, with 'Well, Betsy! How do, Jane?' 'Oh, Mr. Lamb!' they would say, and that was the end of work for that day. He was really rather naughty with the children. One of his tricks was to teach them a new kind of catechism (Mrs. Coe does not remember it, but we may rest assured, I fear, that it was secular), and he made a great fuss with Lizzie Hunt for her skill in saying the Lord's Prayer backwards, which he had taught her.

He had a favourite seat in a tree in the Wilderness at Blakesware, where he would sit and read for hours. Just before meal-times Mrs. Hunt would send the children to tell him to come; but sometimes he preferred to stay there and eat some bread and cheese. He always was particular to return a message either way. 'Give your mother my love and kisses, and say I'll come directly.' Or 'Give your mother my love and kisses, and say I'll eat her beautiful luncheon here.' Adding, 'Don't forget the kisses, whatever you do.'

Mrs. Coe remembers perfectly Blakesware as it used to be. It was only partly destroyed in her young days. She recollects particularly the figure of Nebuchadnezzar eating grass, in one of the pieces of tapestry, with his long fingers like bird's claws. It was one of the great treats for the children to pretend to take rides in the state coach, which Lamb's friend, John Lily, the postilion (mentioned in the poem 'Going or Gone'), had often driven.

At other times Mr. Lamb would watch the trout in the stream, and perhaps feed them, for half the morning. Once or twice he took a rod, but he could never bring himself to fix the worms. 'Barbarous,' he used to say, 'barbarous.'

(It was one of the proudest days of my life, let me interpolate here, when in a lecture on Lamb which the late Sir Walter Raleigh delivered at *The Times* Book Club, I heard him read in his enjoying confidential voice some of the foregoing passages.)

Whether the Misses Norris began at Goddard

House and Lamb miscalled it a 'hovel', or whether they moved into Goddard House later, I cannot say. But if Lamb's word was correct, then they must have moved, for Goddard House still stands for all to see. We are brought into touch with it in a reminiscent poem by Lady Buckmaster, who was born at Widford, published in 1911 under the title of 'My Native Village'. I quote a few lines:

> There is a village little known,
> That in my memory o'ergrown,
> Will ever stand out quite alone;
> For there—the reason you may scorn—
> There stands the house where I was born. . . .

> Now in this little village blest
> One house I ever loved the best,
> (Charles Lamb stayed in it as a guest),

> 'Twas built in day of Good Queen Anne,
> I write of it as best I can;
> 'Twas red like others of that date,
> And had the sweetest garden gate,
> A little wrought-iron work of art,
> A joy to every artist's heart. . . .

> No matter what the time of year,
> The finest flowers were always here;
> A holly hedge grew with such bounty,
> Its fame was spread all through the county;
> And oh! the apples, cherries, pears,
> What colour and what taste was theirs!

When I went down to Widford in the spring of 1932, I found Goddard House shining with new paint on its woodwork and its fences: a symmetrical red-brick residence with a very attractive pediment over the door. Never was there less of a 'hovel'. In the churchyard I found the grave of Mrs. Randal Norris and of Mrs. Coe's father, Thomas Hunt the water-miller, and of Lamb's grandmother, Mary Field (spelt Feild by the mason). But I could not find Abigail Ives, who perhaps was too lowly for a headstone; nor could I decide in my mind as to which was the cottage in this pretty village where she once sold Gibraltar rock.

The next reference to the Widford family in the Lamb correspondence after 1827 comes in 1830, when we find Lamb informing Sarah Hazlitt that the Norris who had just been made Treasurer of the Inner Temple was not, as she had hoped, Dick, but another man of the same name. He adds that, according to the last advices, in 1829, the family were well. There was no more Norris news from Lamb until 1833, when he wrote to Mrs. Norris sending her some books and thanking her for three agreeable days: one of the visits which Mrs. Coe recollected.

Lamb died in 1834, and poor deaf Richard in 1836 and was buried at Widford. Mary Lamb, however, survived, and on Christmas Day, 1841, we find her writing from 41 Alpha Road, Regent's Park, where she was still in the care of Miss James, to Miss Jane Norris:

MY DEAR JANE,

Many thanks for your kind present—your Michaelmas goose. I thought Mr. Moxon had written to thank you—the turkeys and nice apples came yesterday.

Give my love to your dear Mother. I was unhappy to find your note in the basket, for I am always thinking of you all, and wondering when I shall ever see any of you again.

I long to show you what a nice snug place I have got into—in the midst of a pleasant little garden. I have a room for myself and my old books on the ground floor, and a little bedroom up two pairs of stairs. When you come to town, if you have not time to go [to] the Moxons, an Omnibus from the Bell and Crown in Holborn would [bring] you to our door in [a] quarter of an hour. If your dear Mother does not venture so far, I will contrive to pop down to see [her]. Love and all seasonable wishes to your sister and Mary, &c. . . .

If the lodger is gone, I shall have a bedroom will hold two! Heaven bless and preserve you all in health and happiness many a long year.'

In October 1842, Mary Lamb wrote again, with thanks for another goose—'The two legs fell to my share. Your chearful [letter,] my Jane, made me feel "almost as good as new". Your mother and I *must meet again*. Do not be surprized if I pop in again for a half-hour's call some fine frosty morning.'

A year later Mrs. Norris died, aged seventy-eight. Mary Lamb was not well enough herself to write and Miss James therefore wrote for her, again to Jane Norris. The date is July 25, 1843:

MADAM,

Miss Lamb, having seen the Death of your dear Mother in *The Times* News Paper, is most anxious to hear from or to see one of you, as she wishes to know how you intend settling yourselves, and to have a full account of your dear Mother's last illness. She was much shocked on reading of her death, and appeared very vexed that she had not been to see her, [and] wanted very much to come down and see you both; but we were really afraid to let her take the journey. If either of you are coming up to town, she would be glad if you would call upon her, but should you not be likely to come soon, she would be very much pleased if one of you would have the goodness to write a few lines to her, as she is most anxious about you. She begs you to excuse her writing to you herself, as she don't feel equal to it; she asked me yesterday to write for her. I am happy to say she is at present pretty well, although your dear Mother's death appears to dwell much upon her mind. She desires her kindest love to you both, and hopes to hear from you very soon, if you are equal to writing. I sincerely hope you will oblige her, and am,

Madam,

Your obedient, &c.,
SARAH JAMES

Pray don't invite her to come down to see you.

After their mother's death, both the daughters married. Their husbands were local farmers and were brothers: Charles Tween and Arthur Tween. Subsequently, when a wealthy relative of the Norris family named Faint died, the two ladies inherited an independent competency. Just as Craig and I, in 1902, sought out Mrs. Coe, so had Canon Ainger, in 1881, sought out the Mrs. Tweens—Elizabeth, who became Mrs. Charles, and Jane, who became Mrs. Arthur—and was fortunate to find Mrs. Charles. The very charming account of his conversations with her will be found in 'Charles Lamb in Hertfordshire' in his *Lectures and Essays*. Mrs. Tween not only had her memories of Lamb; she had two presentation copies of the *Poetry for Children*, no fewer than three copies of the

Poetical Pieces of John Lamb, and a specimen of his ability, mentioned in his son's essay, as a moulder of heads in clay or plaster of Paris. The Canon made a double appeal to the old lady, first as a Lamb enthusiast, and second the Master of the Temple, where she had been born and brought up. She still bought many of her household necessities from a shop in Fleet Street, just opposite the Temple, for old times' sake.

One thing that Canon Ainger does not seem to have asked Mrs. Tween—about which I want to know more—is the actual reason why the Norrises—herself, her sister, her mother, and poor deaf Richard—objected, as it is always understood that they did, to the account of Randal Norris appearing under the title 'A Death-Bed' in the second *Elia* volume. There is nothing in it but good and the names are disguised. R. N. becomes N. R., Richard becomes Robert, and Charley becomes Jemmy. The accepted theory is that Mrs. Norris did not like the publicity given to her poverty. But why, then, had she not objected when, in 1827, the letter made its first appearance in print in Hone's *Table Book*? Had she done so then, Lamb could never have reprinted it in 1833. Nor need her disapproval have applied to any-

31

thing but the last few lines, after the character sketch was completed. There was, however, sufficient adverse criticism from some quarter or another to cause Lamb, or possibly his publisher, Edward Moxon, to remove 'A Death-Bed' from the volume, and, when in 1835 a second edition was called for, to substitute for it that lurid and disturbing fantasy 'Confessions of a Drunkard', which had been written as long ago as 1813.

Canon Ainger, I may add, was not the only student of Lamb to visit the Tweens. Carew Hazlitt also did so, bringing away Charles Tween's testimony that 'Mr. Lamb had so small and "immaterial" a figure that when out walking with him he used to put his hands under his arms and lift him over a stile as if he were nothing'.

It is through the courtesy of Mr. C. W. B. Richardson, a descendant by marriage of Charles Tween, that I am able to publish the reproduction of Randal Norris's portrait, which to my eye has a fine air of rugged benevolence. The original is a miniature dated 1816, and the fact that the painter of it was Matilda Betham gives it further interest, for she was of the Lamb circle too.

Matilda Betham, the daughter of a Suffolk

parson, was a year younger than Lamb, and she survived him until 1852. In addition to making likenesses, she wrote poetry and compiled a biographical dictionary of famous women. Every one seems to have liked her, and Lamb's praises of her *Lay of Marie* should have been intoxicating to her. But he would not allow her to do his face, although Coleridge had submitted to the ordeal. His first refusal was in 1808, and I feel sure there were others. Nor in 1815 could he find time to go through the artist's poem; but to be the recipient of such excuses as follow should, for the poet, have been gratification enough:

. . . My head is in such a state from incapacity for business that I certainly know it to be my duty not to undertake the veriest trifle in addition. I hardly know how to go on. I have tried to get some redress by explaining my health, but with no great success. No one can tell how ill I am, because it does not come out to the exterior of my face, but lies in my skull deep and invisible. I wish I was leprous and black jaundiced skin-over, and that all was as well within as my cursed looks. You must not think me worse than I am. I am determined not to be overset, but to give up business rather and get 'em to allow me a trifle for services past. O that I had been a shoe-maker or a baker, or a man of large independent fortune. O darling Laziness! heaven of Epicurus! Saints

Everlasting Rest! that I could drink vast potations of thee thro' unmeasured Eternity. Otium *cum* vel *sine* dignitate. Scandalous, dishonourable, any-kind-of-*repose*. I stand not upon the *dignified sort*. Accursed damned desks, trade, commerce, business—Inventions of that old original busy body brainworking Satan, sabbathless restless Satan—

A curse relieves. Do you ever try it?

Although Lamb did not want his own countenance limned, he was busy in Miss Betham's interest. In 1816, the year in which the Randal Norris miniature was made, Mary Lamb was writing to Sarah Hutchinson, Wordsworth's sister-in-law (or 'third wife', as Lamb called her):

. . . Do you think Mr. Wordsworth would have any reluctance to write (strongly recommending to their patronage) to any of his rich friends in London to solicit employment for Miss Betham as a Miniature Painter? If you give me hopes that he will not be averse to do this, I will write to you more fully stating the infinite good he would do by performing so irksome a task as I know asking favours to be . . .

to which Charles Lamb adds:

. . . I just snatch the Pen out of my sister's hand to finish rapidly. Wordswth. may tell De Q

34

that Miss B's price for a Virgin and Child is three guineas.

Bearing these remarks in mind, I should say it is more than likely that it was Lamb's commendation of Miss Betham's skill which led to this miniature of Randal Norris being painted at all. 'He did many kind things like that.'

1932

THE FRONTISPIECE

FOR too long the Benchers of the Inner Temple withheld any recognition of the honour done them when the author of *Elia* chose Crown Office Row, facing their garden, as his birthplace. But at last a tablet was set up on the house, and in 1930 this was followed by a statue of a boy at the edge of a fish-pond, on the lawn of the garden, near enough to the Embankment for the unprivileged, peering through the railing, to see. He is a pretty boy, clasping a book, on the open page of which you may read these words from a famous essay: 'Lawyers were children once . . .'

We owe the idea of the memorial to the imagination of the Master of the Garden and the actual workmanship to Miss Margaret Wrightson. At first I thought the boy might be meant to be the youthful Elia himself; but the very marked want of aquilinity in the nose and the fact that he is reading something written by himself thirty or more years later made that impossible.

1933

THE WINGED HORSE

IN the essay on 'The Old Benchers of the Inner Temple', written in 1821, Lamb says:

They have lately gothicized the entrance to the Inner Temple Hall, and the library front, to assimilate them, I suppose, to the body of the hall, which they do not at all resemble. What is become of the winged horse that stood over the former? a stately arms! and who has removed those frescoes of the Virtues, which Italianized the end of the Paper-buildings?—my first hint of allegory! They must account to me for these things, which I miss so greatly.

In the very informative book of annotations on this essay which Sir F. D. Mackinnon, himself a Master of the Bench of the Inner Temple, issued through the Clarendon Press in 1927, there is the following note on the passage I have quoted:

I know of no picture showing this [the Winged Horse], and I do not know what became of it. In the upper part of the modern turret staircase to the Library there are set up two examples of the winged horse in stone, removed from old

THE WINGED HORSE
From the Marble Relief, probably by J. M. Rysbrack,
on the Library Staircase of the Inner Temple

buildings, but neither is the one from over the entrance to the old Hall.

Of one of these Winged Horses I have been permitted by the Treasurer of the Inner Temple to print a photograph. It is a noble animal—'a stately arms' indeed—attributed by Mrs. Arundel Esdaile, our leading authority on the sculpture of that period, to J. M. Rysbrack (1694–1770), a Dutch sculptor who was working in England at the same time as Roubilliac and Scheemakers, and whose hand is to be found in many of our memorials, one of the best known being his bust of John Gay in Westminster Abbey, with its epitaph by Pope and Gay's own flippant couplet.

1933

THE EVOLUTION OF WHIMSICALITY

THE title shall stand, because I like it; but it does not say all. By whimsicality, I ought to explain, I mean, broadly, modern humour, as distinguished from that which we find before the end of the eighteenth century. It may comprise all the earlier forms, but it is different, perhaps in its very blending, and it has one ingredient which the older forms lacked, and which, like the onion in the bowl of salad, as celebrated by one of its masters—Sydney Smith—'animates the whole'. I refer to its unreluctant egoism. It is this auto-biographical quality that is its most noticeable characteristic—the author's side-long amused canonization of himself; his frankly shameless assumption that if a thing is interesting to the writer it must therefore be of interest to the world. And with the development of whimsicality (as I call it) are bound up also the development of slippered ease in literature and the stages by which we have all become funnier. To-day every one can grow the flower, with more or less success, for every one has the seed.

Although the new humour comprises the old, it has never reached its predecessor's heights in certain of its branches. Only in parody and nonsense have we gained. There has, for example, been no modern satire to equal Pope's and Dryden's and Swift's; no irony more biting than Swift's and Defoe's, or more delicate and ingratiating than Goldsmith's; no such cynical or grotesque humour as Shakespeare exults in; no rough-and-tumble buffoonery like Fielding's and Smollett's. In nonsense and in parody alone we have improved, the old days having nothing to offer to be compared with Lewis Carroll or that can surpass Calverley; but in burlesque we cannot compete with *The Rehearsal*, *The Beggar's Opera*, or *The Critic*.

But all the authors I have named were impersonal. They suppressed themselves. We have no evidence as to whether Shakespeare was more like Falstaff or Prospero; probably he resembled both, but we cannot know. Goldsmith is the only autobiographer among them, but even he always affected to be some one else; he had not the courage of the first person singular, and Steele and Addison, eminently fitted as they were to inaugurate the new era, clung to tradition and employed a stalking horse. Even Sterne only pretended to be himself, although whimsicality in the strictest meaning of the word undoubtedly was his.

The period when whimsicality came in—the end of the eighteenth and beginning of the nineteenth century—was the period when a return to nature in poetry was in gestation; a movement beginning subconsciously with Cowper and Crabbe and finding its most eloquent conscious prophets in Wordsworth and Coleridge, and its gospel in the preface to the second edition of the *Lyrical Ballads* in 1800. Coleridge and Wordsworth were the great wave. Beneath the impressive surface of the ocean which they disturbed and crested, in the calm waters where letter-writing is carried on (if I may be pardoned not the best of metaphors), the other development was in progress; correspondents were becoming more familiar. I would not allege that humour and the epistolary art were strangers until, say, 1780—there is, indeed, very good evidence to the contrary—but it was somewhere about that time that a more conscious facetiousness crept in, and just as Wordsworth's revolutionary methods held the field and ousted the heightened conventional language of the eighteenth-century poets, so did this new and natural levity gain strength. Hitherto men had divided themselves strictly between their light moods and their grave moods. But gradually these were allowed to mingle, and in course of time quite serious people let their pens frisk as merrily as the professional wags.

It was left for Charles Lamb so to confuse *déshabillé* and full dress that after him no author had any rigid need to keep them apart; but Lamb was not the fountain head. He had a predecessor; and we come to that predecessor, the real father of whimsicality, the first writer of our modern humorous prose, in a phrase in a letter of Lamb's on December 5, 1796—thus keeping the chain intact. Writing to Coleridge, Lamb refers to Cowper's 'divine chit-chat', and although that phrase no doubt applied to 'Table Talk' and 'The Task' and other poetical monologues, we may here borrow it to describe the ease and fun and unaffected egoism which in Cowper's letters are for the first time found in perfection in English literature. As early as 1778 he was writing like this (to William Unwin) :

> We are indebted to you for your political intelligence, but have it not in our power to pay you in kind. Proceed, however, to give us such information as cannot be learned from the newspaper; and when anything arises at Olney, that is not in

the threadbare style of daily occurrences, you shall hear of it in return. Nothing of this sort has happened lately, except that a lion was imported here at the fair, seventy years of age, and was as tame as a goose. Your mother and I saw him embrace his keeper with his paws, and lick his face. Others saw him receive his head in his mouth, and restore it to him again unhurt—a sight we chose not to be favoured with, but rather advised the honest man to discontinue the practice—a practice hardly reconcilable to prudence, unless he had a head to spare.

In 1779, again to William Unwin:

I remember,—(the fourth and last thing I mean to remember on this occasion), that Sam Cox, the Counsel, walking by the seaside as if absorbed in deep contemplation, was questioned about what he was musing on. He replied, 'I was wondering that such an almost infinite and unwieldy element should produce a *sprat*.'

And again, concerning a man named Twopenny:

It seems a trifle, but it is a real disadvantage to have no better name to pass by than the gentleman you mention. Whether we suppose him settled, and promoted in the army, the Church, or the law, how uncouth the sound—Captain Twopenny! Bishop Twopenny! Judge Twopenny! The abilities of Lord Mansfield would hardly impart a dignity to such a name. Should he

44

THE EVOLUTION OF WHIMSICALITY

perform deeds worthy of poetical panegyric, how difficult it would be to ennoble the sound of Twopenny!

> Muse! place him high upon the lists of Fame,
> The wondrous man, and Twopenny his name!

But to be serious, if the French should land in the Isle of Thanet, and Mr. Twopenny should fall into their hands, he will have a fair opportunity to frenchify his name, and may call himself Monsieur Deux Sous; which, when he comes to be exchanged by Cartel, will easily resume an English form, and slide naturally into Two Shoes, in my mind a considerable improvement.

In 1780, with a copy of verses, to the same correspondent:

> I shall charge you a half-penny apiece for every copy I send you, the short as well as the long. This is a sort of afterclap you little expected, but I cannot possibly afford them at a cheaper rate. If this method of raising money had occurred to me sooner, I should have made the bargain sooner; but am glad I have hit upon it at last. It will be a considerable encouragement to my muse, and act as a powerful stimulus to my industry. If the American war should last much longer I may be obliged to raise my price.

Such passages as these, limpid, unaffected, setting down daily trivialities as carefully and amusingly as was in the author's power, seem to me to mark the beginnings of much modern humour. There are hints of the same quality in Swift, in Walpole and in Gray, but those writers are of their own time, and to us they are often archaic. Cowper was the first to handle the new prose, although he did not come out into the open with it. He was, publicly, a poet, and was read for his poetry. The innovating work that he had begun, if it was to prosper, needed a public writer to make it generally acceptable, and such was Charles Lamb. If Cowper was the father of whimsicality, Lamb was its chief popularizer.

Lamb's great discovery was that he himself was better worth laying bare than obscuring: that his memories, his impressions, his loyalties, his dislikes, his doubts, his beliefs, his prejudices, his enthusiasms, in short, everything that was his, were suitable material for literature. Pope said that the proper study of mankind was man; Lamb amended this to—the proper study of man is himself. If you know yourself and have confidence in your moods and general sagacity, a record is worth making. Addison and Steele had even better opportunities to be disclosing than Lamb: they had a daily paper, and could write every morning exactly what they liked, and often must have been so hard put to it for subjects that autobiography would seem to be the easy way; yet they were always inventing. The time for personal confidences had not come.

But whether Lamb would have been as he is without these forerunners is a question. In so far as the modernity of his humour is concerned, I think that he would, but no doubt his early contributions to *The Reflector*, some ten years before *Elia*, were based on the old models. Years, however, before he wrote those (in 1811) for print, he had, for private friendly eyes only, penned in his letters such passages as this (in April 1800, to Coleridge):

You read us a dismal homily upon 'Realities'! We know, quite as well as you do, what are shadows and what are realities. You, for instance, when you are over your fourth or fifth jorum, chirping about old school occurrences, are the best of realities. Shadows are cold, thin things, that have no warmth or grasp in them. Miss Wesley and her friend, and a tribe of authoresses that come after you here daily, and, in defect of you, hive and cluster upon us, are the shadows. You encouraged that mopsey, Miss Wesley, to dance after you, in the hope of having her nonsense put into a nonsensical Anthology. We have pretty well shaken her off, by that simple expedient of referring her to you; but there are more burrs in the wind.

I came home t'other day from business, hungry as a hunter, to dinner, with nothing, I am sure, of *the author but hunger* about me, and whom found I closeted with Mary but a friend of this Miss Wesley—one Miss Benje, or Benjey—I don't know how she spells her name. I just came in time enough, I believe, luckily to prevent them from exchanging vows of eternal friendship. It seems she is one of your authoresses, that you first foster, and then upbraid us with. But I forgive you. 'The rogue has given me potions to make me love him.' Well; go she would not, nor step a step over our threshold, till we had promised to come and drink tea with her next night. I had never seen her before, and could not tell who the devil it was that was so familiar.

We went, however, not to be impolite. Her lodgings are up two pairs of stairs in East Street. Tea and coffee, and macaroons—a kind of cake I much love. We sat down. Presently Miss Benje broke the silence, by declaring herself quite of a different opinion from D'Israeli, who supposes the differences of human intellect to be the mere effect of organization. She begged to know my opinion. I attempted to carry it off with a pun upon organ; but that went off very flat. She immediately conceived a very low opinion of my metaphysics; and turning round to Mary, put some question to her in French—possibly having heard that neither Mary nor I understood French.

The explanation that took place occasioned some embarrassment and much wondering.

She then fell into an insulting conversation about the comparative genius and merits of all modern languages, and concluded with asserting that the Saxon was esteemed the purest dialect in Germany. From thence she passed into the subject of poetry; where I, who had hitherto sat mute and a hearer only, humbly hoped I might now put in a word to some advantage, seeing that it was my own trade in a manner. But I was stopped by a round assertion that no good poetry had appeared since Dr. Johnson's time. It seems the Doctor has suppressed many hopeful geniuses that way by the severity of his critical strictures in his *Lives of the Poets*. I here ventured to question the fact, and was beginning to appeal to *names*, but I was assured 'it was certainly the case'. Then we discussed Miss More's book on education, which I had never read. . . .

It being now nine o'clock, wine and macaroons were again served round, and we parted, with a promise to go again next week and meet the Miss Porters, who, it seems, have heard much of Mr. Coleridge, and wish to meet *us*, because we are *his* friends. I have been preparing for the occasion. I crowd cotton in my ears. I read all the reviews and magazines of the past month against the dreadful meeting, and I hope by these means to cut a tolerable second-rate figure.

I can find nothing quite like that, so humorous, and rapid, in any writer before

Lamb. There is hardly an antiquated word in it. But what is more interesting about it is that no one hitherto would have thought the narration worth while. That, perhaps, is the most significant thing.

After another example from the same year, 1800, the account of Joseph Cottle (author of *Alfred*) being gradually wooed from his grief for his brother Amos Cottle's death, I shall have quoted enough.

> I suppose you have heard of the death of Amos Cottle.
>
> I paid a solemn visit of condolence to his brother, accompanied by George Dyer, of burlesque memory. I went, trembling to see poor Cottle so immediately upon the event.
>
> He was in black; and his younger brother was also in black.
>
> Everything wore an aspect suitable to the respect due to the freshly dead. For some time after our entrance nobody spoke, till George modestly put in a question, whether *Alfred* was likely to sell.
>
> This was *Lethe* to Cottle, and his poor face, wet with tears, and his kind eye, brightened up in a moment. Now I felt it was my cue to speak.
>
> I had to thank him for a present of a magnificent copy, and had promised to send him my remarks, —the least thing I could do; so I ventured to suggest, that I perceived a considerable improvement he had made in his first book since the state

in which he first read it to me. Joseph until now
had sat with his knees cowering in by the fireplace,
and with great difficulty of body shifted the same
round to the corner of a table where I was sitting,
and first stationing one thigh over the other,
which is his sedentary mood, and placidly fixing
his benevolent face right against mine, waited
my observations.

At that moment it came strongly into my mind,
that I had got Uncle Toby before me, he looked
so kind and good.

I could not say an unkind thing of *Alfred*. So
I set my memory to work to recollect what was
the name of Alfred's Queen, and with some
adroitness recalled the well-known sound to
Cottle's ears of Alswitha.

At that moment I could perceive that Cottle
had forgot his brother was so lately become a
blessed spirit. In the language of mathematicians,
the author was as 9, the brother as 1.

I felt my cue, and strong pity working at the
root I went to work, and beslabbered *Alfred*
with most unqualified praise, or only qualifying
my praise by the occasional politic interposition
of an exception taken against trivial faults, slips,
and human imperfections, which, by removing
the appearance of insincerity, did but in truth
heighten the relish.

Perhaps I might have spared that refinement,
for Joseph was in a humour to hope and believe
all things.

What I said was beautifully supported, corro-
borated and confirmed by the stupidity of his

brother on my left hand, and by George on my right, who has an utter incapacity of comprehending that there can be anything bad in poetry,

All poems are *good* poems to George; all men are *fine geniuses*.

So, what with my actual memory, of which I made the most, and Cottle's own helping me out —for I had really forgotten a good deal of *Alfred* —I made shift to discuss the most essential part, entirely to the satisfaction of its author, who repeatedly declared that he loved nothing better than *candid* criticism. Was I a candid greyhound now for all this? or did I do right? I believe I did. The effect was luscious to my conscience.

For all the rest of the evening Amos was no more heard of, till George revived the subject by inquiring whether some account should not be drawn up by the friends of the deceased to be inserted in Phillips' *Monthly Obituary*; adding, that Amos was estimable both for his head and heart, and would have made a fine poet if he had lived.

To the expediency of this measure Cottle fully assented, but could not help adding that he always thought that the qualities of his brother's heart exceeded those of his head.

I believe his brother, when living, had formed precisely the same idea of him; and I apprehend the world will assent to both judgments.

One feels that the man who could be writing with such sureness and zest as that in the year

1800 ought to have come to his *Elia* vein—
1820—sooner. But the clock always has to
strike first.

Puns in their absurd latter-day form also
were coming in in the same decade that gave
us the *Lyrical Ballads*. There had been puns
before—Shakespeare has many, and Swift and
Doctor Sheridan rejoiced in exchanging them—
but they were less light-hearted, more verbal;
the pun with nonsense to it, such as we associate
first with Lamb, is not earlier than he. In a
magazine published in 1793 (when Lamb was
eighteen) I find this fragment of history gravely
set forth: 'When the seamen on board the ship
of Christopher Columbus came in sight of San
Salvador they burst out into exuberant mirth
and jollity. "The lads are in a merry key,"
cried the commodore. America is now the
name of half the globe.' That is less like
the eighteenth century than the century that
was to produce Hood and H. J. Byron and
F. C. Burnand.

Before *Elia*, no one writing for print had
assumed that his own impressions of life, grave
and gay, were a sufficient or even a suitable
subject. Such self-analytical authors as there
had been had selected and garnished according
to the canons of taste of their time. Lamb came

naturally to his task and fondled and displayed his ego with all the ecstasy of a collector exhibiting bric-à-brac or first editions; and ever since then, acting upon his sanction, others have been doing it. But what has at the moment the most interest to me is that part of Lamb's legacy which embodies his freakish humour; it was his willingness to be naturally funny that has benefited so many heirs. I should say that his principal service to other writers lay in giving them, by his example, encouragement to be their age (as the American slang has it), to mix their comic fancies with their serious thoughts as they are mixed in real life. The mingled thread, he showed, should never be divided.

The influence of letters must not be stressed; for the examples from Lamb were written before he could have seen any of Cowper's correspondence, while none of Lamb's letters were made public until Talfourd's memoir of him in 1837. But although Lamb could not be influenced by Cowper's prose until 1804—nor needed to be, then—he was stimulated by the 'divine chit-chat' of his verse, which brought a happy egoism into general popularity. He then developed and simmered for a couple of decades, and the next great event in the evolution of whimsicality was the outcome of those comparatively silent years, the *Elia* essays beginning in the *London Magazine* in 1820.

Thus we have four notable years: 1782, Cowper's first *Poems*—'Table Talk,' etc.; 1785, *The Task* (with 'John Gilpin'); 1804, new edition of Hayley's *Life of Cowper*, with correspondence added; 1820, *Elia* essays begin.

I am not suggesting any conscious derivation from Lamb in modern writers. To begin with, no writer who is an imitator can be worth anything, for obviously he lacks pride; but a writer can be both an individual and under influence. He can move on parallel lines with his predecessor, not intentionally, but through a similarity of outlook. It would be absurd, in spite of his own admission with regard to sedulous apishness, to say, for example, that Stevenson imitated Lamb; but what one may contend is that but for the new easy familiar personal turn which Lamb gave to literature, Stevenson's *Inland Voyage* and *Travels with a Donkey* might never have been written. Their derivation is more commonly given to Sterne's *Sentimental Journey* and, in so far as form goes, possibly with accuracy; but although the mould may be from Sterne, for the nature of the contents we are far more indebted to Lamb. Sterne was an

affected piece, posturing and grimacing too
often; but Lamb, who is always divulging, was
above pretence, and the example which he set
to writers coming after him was courage to be
themselves and to be all of themselves all the
time.

Meanwhile, during the period when Lamb
was writing Addisonian exercises for *The
Reflector*, and preparing to be himself and
nothing but himself ever after, a little boy
was born—the year was 1812, and the date
February 7—in an obscure house in an obscure
part of Portsmouth. His father was a dockyard
clerk, named John Dickens, and the little boy
was christened Charles John Huffam, but the
John and the Huffam quickly disappeared and
Charles only remained. This boy, who was
destined not only to delight the world into
which he was projected, but to create a new
world of his own, was, I am sure, fired by
Lamb's example. Dickens himself tells us that
among his childish reading was *Elia*, which had
begun in the *London Magazine* when he was
eight. The other little Charles could thus have
read, at the most impressionable age, the
account of Ralph Bigod, the Micawberesque
borrower of money, and of Jem White, who
had such a glorious Dickensian way at the

chimney-sweeps' suppers. Even genius often has to be put in the right path. If it is admitted that Lamb influenced Dickens, then my point is firmly enough established, for Dickens was the first really comic writer that we have had, and his own influence must have been endless. Before Dickens, no author had tried to be as funny as he could, or at any rate no author had done so with any acceptance.

Cowper, then, and Lamb (with Walpole and Gray as less guilty accomplices) must be convicted of the sweet offence of bringing whimsicality into literature and making it all the easier for our own artists in that medium to earn a living.

1922

TWO ONE-LEGGED MEN
WITH AN ASIDE ON THE TEMPLE

I WAS astonished in Norfolk Street, off the
Strand, one morning, to find a one-legged
man, dressed in spotless singlet and shorts,
leaping a pole which he had poised at the side
of the road. Although furnished with only a
moiety of our normal jumping apparatus, he
cleared great heights, and the passers-by were
far more generous in their contributions to his
cap than often we are to screevers and street
musicians. This was early in the day—about
ten o'clock—and if he was to continue to earn
his living like that until dewy eve he would
need to be a very strong fellow. He seemed, so
to speak, to bring to life the American simile:
'As busy as a one-legged man in a forest fire.'
And could there be a more curious or strenuous
mode of livelihood? The woman in Virginia
who amassed a fortune by taking the curl out
of negresses' hair had seemed to follow as odd
a career as any that I knew; but for a one-
legged man to thrive on jumping—that is
almost as remarkable as the success of the

one-armed juggler in *The Wallet of Kai Lung*.

The unusual acrobat of Norfolk Street did me an intellectual service by reminding me of one of Goldsmith's best satirical papers and sending me again to the works of that perfect writer. One of the sadder things of life is our inability to keep up with our favourite authors of the past, except on the principle of reading an old book to mark the arrival of a new. But that is a procedure of perfection. The ordinary person, even when a member of what is called the leisured class, cannot be as negligent of the thoughts and manners of his own time as to follow so superior an example; while busy people who were always thus ringing in the old would know nothing of current literature at all. Hence it is that not for far too long have I had a volume of Goldsmith in my hand.

The particular bloom of little Goldy's whimsical and quizzical genius that I was seeking was that sly and most admirable exercise in irony, "The History of the Distresses of an English Disabled Soldier," because the simple figure there revealed had, like my Norfolk Street friend (who was probably an ex-Service man himself), but one original leg left: the missing article, in his case, being supplied by wood. Let me condense the narrative of this poor fellow's misfortunes.

At his father's death the boy was put into a workhouse, where he led an easy kind of life for five years. 'I wrought', he says, 'only ten hours in the day.' Then becoming a wandering labourer, he was so unlucky as to kill a hare belonging to a J.P. and was sent by the J.P. to Newgate in order to be transported as a vagabond. 'People may say this and that of being in jail; but, for my part, I found Newgate as agreeable a place as ever in my life.' Imprisonment was, however, too good to last, and after five months he was put on board a ship, with two hundred more, for the plantations. 'We had but an indifferent passage, for, being all confined in the hold, more than a hundred of our people died for want of sweet air, and these that remained were sickly enough, God knows.'

After seven years labouring for a planter among negroes, our hero's time expired and he worked his way home. 'I was glad to see Old England again, because I loved my country.' Not long after, however, he was knocked down by the press-gang, and forced to become a soldier, served two campaigns in Flanders, was at Val and Fontenoy, and received a wound in the chest. He then enlisted as a landsman in the East India Company's service and fought the French in six pitched battles. 'I verily believe that if I could read or write, our captain would have made me a corporal.'

Before his vessel could reach home he was pressed for a sailor, captured by the French, and imprisoned in Brest. 'I hate the French because they are all slaves and wear wooden shoes.' He and some companions, escaping from jail, seized a boat and got out of the harbour, but only to be taken by the Dorset privateer and forced to join its crew. 'In three days we fell in with the *Pompadour* privateer of forty guns, while we had but twenty-three; so to it we went, yard-arm and yard-arm. I verily believe we should have taken the Frenchmen, had we but had some more men left behind; but unfortunately we lost all our men just as we were going to get the victory.' (Here we find Goldsmith anticipating a later satirist, W. S. Gilbert. The sailor's song in *Ruddigore*, emphasizing French inferiority at sea, is very much in the same manner.)

The soldier continues: 'I had almost forgot to tell you that in that engagement I was wounded in two places. I lost four fingers of the left hand and my leg was shot off. If I had

had the good fortune to have lost my leg and
the use of my hand on board a King's ship,
and not aboard a privateer, I should have been
entitled to clothing and maintenance during
the rest of my life. But that was not my chance:
one man is born with a silver spoon in his
mouth and another with a wooden ladle.
However, blessed be God! I enjoy good health,
and will ever love liberty and Old England.
Liberty, property, and Old England for ever,
huzza!'

Any reader of these passages who is sent to
the shelves to take down Oliver Goldsmith and
renew acquaintance with him is to be envied.
And particularly if he alights upon *The Citizen
of the World*. He will then meet the Man in
Black and Beau Tibbs, and Mrs. Tibbs, and
the Chinese Philosopher with his deadly pene-
tration. And everywhere he will find humanity,
humour, and the most easy and charming of
literary styles.

As I stood beside Goldsmith's plain slab at
the side of the Temple Church a day or so
after re-reading these essays, it occurred to me
that it was a curious chance that made this
abode of lawyers the home of the two English
writers of the eighteenth century who are most
beloved. For Oliver Goldsmith lived for some

years in Garden Court, and later at 2, Brick Court, and died there on April 4, 1774, and Charles Lamb was born on February 10, 1775, at 2, Crown Office Row, only a stone's throw away, and lodged later both in Mitre Court Buildings and Inner Temple Lane.

And the Temple's association with the more personal and benignly smiling side of literature does not end there. A later tenant of the Brick Court rooms was one William Makepeace Thackeray, author of the *Roundabout Papers* and the first to call Lamb 'Saint Charles'.

1929

LAMB AND THE UNIVERSITIES

CAMBRIDGE did more for Lamb than is perhaps recognized even on the banks of the Cam, where most things are known, although Lamb did less for Cambridge than he should have done—as we shall see. Cambridge indeed played no small part in his life, for it gave him not only his intimacy with Manning, which brought forth to their full for the first time, and at a very critical time, his powers of humorous improvisation and led to some of the richest letters in the language; but it also gave him his adopted daughter Emma Isola, without whom his old age, often sad enough as it was, would have been sadder.

Lamb's first link with Cambridge was Coleridge. Coleridge came hither—to Jesus College —from Christ's Hospital and Lamb's company in February 1791. He left Cambridge (without a degree) and returned to Lamb's company late in 1794, and at once they set to writing sonnets together. Lamb, I think, visited Cambridge in Coleridge's time, staying with another Christ's Hospitaller, Frederick William Franklin; but of the date of this visit we have no record.

His second link with Cambridge was George Dyer, who spent a large part of his laborious life in compiling valuable if unexciting works in connexion with the University; but that of course was indirect. Writing to Manning in 1800, Lamb says:

> Send me some news from the *banks of Cam*, as the poets delight to speak, especially George Dyer, who has no other name, nor idea, nor definition of Cambridge—namely, its being a market-town, sending members to Parliament, never entered into his definition: it was and is, simply the banks of the Cam, or the fair Cam, as Oxford is the banks of the Isis, or the fair Isis.

Coleridge and Franklin having left, Lamb would have had no Cambridge tie but for the egregious but useful Charles Lloyd, who, after quarrelling with Coleridge, defying his father, and marrying against the advice of most of his own and his wife's friends, had in 1799 settled down there to study. Requiring a tutor, his footsteps were led by a wise providence to a strange mathematical recluse—famous in his cups for his comic grimaces—named Thomas Manning. Manning was then twenty-seven. He had been at Caius from 1790 to 1795, but objecting to oaths and tests he had not taken his degree, and was now leading an odd, ruminative, semi-industrious existence, and waiting for his real purpose in life to be fulfilled: the meeting with a poor London clerk, three years his junior, named Charles Lamb, who by sympathetic appreciation called forth a wealth of freakishness, sagacity, and wit, that otherwise might never have been awakened.

Lamb and Manning were brought together by Lloyd at Birmingham in 1799. It was much the best deed of Lloyd's life; a friendship sprang up instantly; Lloyd dropped out; and the next time that Lamb visited Cambridge it was as Manning's guest, Manning having already stayed with Lamb in London and met Coleridge. The return visit was postponed again and again, but on December 27, 1800, Lamb was able to write in practically certain terms:

> Man of many snipes, I will sup with thee Deo volente, et diabolo nolente, on Monday night, the 5th of January, in the new year, and crush a cup to the infant century.
>
> A word or two of my progress. Embark at six o'clock in the morning, with a fresh gale, on a Cambridge one-decker; very cold till eight at night; land at St. Mary's light-house, muffins and coffee upon table (or any other curious

66

production of Turkey or both Indies), snipes exactly at nine, punch to commence at ten, with *argument*; difference of opinion is expected to take place about eleven; perfect unanimity, with some haziness and dimness, before twelve.—N.B. My single affection is not so singly wedded to snipes; but the curious and epicurean eye would also take a pleasure in beholding a delicate and well-chosen assortment of teals, ortolans, the unctuous and palate-soothing flesh of geese wild and tame, nightingales' brains, the sensorium of a young sucking pig, or any other Christmas dish, which I leave to the judgment of you and the cook of Gonville.

Manning then lived over a barber's in St. Mary's Passage. The barber's name was Crisp, which Lamb preferred to call Crips. It is now Number 3, the premises of Messrs. Kidd & Baker, and, though modernization has occurred, the true Elian may, when there, be thrilled to know that Lamb was once there too, and convivial to boot.

Manning left Cambridge for Paris in 1801, to study Chinese, and everyone must remember that perfect example of fantastic humour based on affection: Lamb's letter dissuading him from settling in China. Before he definitely left Europe, however, Manning seems to have returned to Cambridge for a while, for in 1805 he sent Lamb a brawn, which Lamb, in his acknowledgment, affected to consider was the gift, not of Manning but of Richard Hopkins, the cook of Caius. He writes:

At first I thought of declining the present; but Richard knew my blind side when he pitched upon brawn. 'Tis of all my hobbies the supreme in the eating way. . . . Brawn was a noble thought. It is not every common gullet-fancier that can properly esteem it. It is like a picture of one of the choice old Italian masters. Its gusto is of that hidden sort. As Wordsworth sings of a modest poet,—'you must love him, ere to you he will seem worthy of your love'; so brawn, you must taste it, ere to you it will seem to have any taste at all. But 'tis nuts to the adept: those that will send out their tongues and feelers to find it out. It will be wooed, and not unsought be won. Now, ham-essence, lobsters, turtle, such popular minions, absolutely *court you*, lay themselves out to strike you at first smack, like one of David's pictures . . . compared with the plain russet-coated wealth of a Titian or a Correggio. . . . Such are the obvious glaring heathen virtues of a corporation dinner, compared with the reserved collegiate worth of brawn. Do me the favour to leave off the business which you may be at present upon, and go immediately to the kitchens of Trinity and Caius, and make my most respectful compliments to Mr. Richard Hopkins, and assure him that his brawn is most excellent. . . . I leave it to you whether you shall choose to pay him the civility of asking him to dinner while you stay in Cambridge, or in whatever other way you may best like to show your gratitude to *my friend*. Richard Hopkins, considered in many points of view, is a very extraordinary character. Adieu: I hope to see you to supper in London soon, where we will taste Richard's brawn, and drink his health in a cheerful but moderate cup. We have not many such men in any rank of life as Mr. R. Hopkins.

Cambridge should be proud of that letter, because it contains what might be called the first draft—the seed at any rate—of the Dissertation on Roast Pig (which also we owe to Manning). Cambridge men should be happy to know that it was the cook of Trinity Hall and Caius who first touched Lamb's palate and genius to these fine issues.

With Manning, who left Cambridge for ever in 1805, went the last of the early ties; and it was not till 1815 that Lamb was there again, and then only by chance. We know all about it from a letter—to my mind almost a perfect letter—from Mary Lamb to Miss Hutchinson, Wordsworth's sister-in-law, a large part of which I now quote. The date is August 20, 1815:

Last Saturday was the grand feast day of the India House Clerks. I think you must have heard Charles talk of his yearly turtle feast. He had been lately much wearied with work, and, glad to get rid of all connected with it, he *used* Saturday, the feast day being a holiday, *borrowed* the Monday following, and we set off from the outside of the Cambridge Coach from Fetter Lane at eight o'clock, and were driven into Cambridge in great triumph by Hell-Fire Dick five minutes before three. Richard is in high reputation, he is private tutor to the Whip Club. . . .

In my life I never spent so many pleasant hours together as I did at Cambridge. We were walking the whole time—out of one College into another. If you ask me which I like best I must make the children's traditionary unoffending reply to all curious inquirers—'*Both*'. I liked them all best. The little gloomy ones, because they were little gloomy ones. I felt as if I could live and die in them and never wish to speak again. And the fine grand Trinity College, oh how fine it was! And King's College Chapel, what a place! I heard the Cathedral service there, and having been no great church goer of late years, *that* and the painted windows and the general effect of the whole thing affected me wonderfully.

I certainly like St. John's College best. I had seen least of it, having only been over it once, so, on the morning we returned, I got up at six o'clock and wandered into it by myself—by myself indeed, for there was nothing alive to be seen but one cat, who followed me about like a dog.

Then I went over Trinity, but nothing hailed me there, not even a cat.

On the Sunday we met with a pleasant thing. We had been congratulating each other that we had come alone to enjoy, as the miser his feast, all our sights greedily to ourselves, but having seen all we began to grow flat and wish for this and t'other body with us, when we were accosted by a young gownsman whose face we knew, but where or how we had seen him we could not tell, and were obliged to ask his name. He proved to be a young man we had seen twice at Alsager's. He turned out a very pleasant fellow—shewed us the insides of places—we took him to our Inn to dinner, and drank tea with him in such a delicious College room, and then again he supped with us. We made our meals as short as possible, to lose no time, and walked our young conductor almost off his legs. Even when the fried eels were ready for supper and coming up, having a message from a man who he had bribed for the purpose, that then we might see Oliver Cromwell [Cooper's portrait] who was *not at home* when we called to see him, we sallied out again and made him a visit by candlelight—and so ended our sights. When we were setting out in the morning our new friend came to bid us good-bye, and rode with us as far as Trumpington. I never saw a creature so happy as he was the whole time he was with us, he said we had put him in such good spirits that [he] should certainly pass an examination well that he is to go through in six weeks in order to qualify himself to obtain a fellowship.

Returning home down old Fetter Lane I could hardly keep from crying to think it was all over. With what pleasure [Charles] shewed me Jesus College where Coleridge was—the barbe[r's shop] where Manning was—the house where Lloyd lived —Franklin's rooms, a young schoolfellow with whom Charles was the first time he went to Cambridge: I peeped in at his window, the room looked quite deserted—old chairs standing about in disorder that seemed to have stood there ever since they had sate in them. I write sad nonsense about these things, but I wish you had heard Charles talk his nonsense over and over again about his visit to Franklin and how he then first felt himself commencing gentleman and had eggs for his breakfast.

Lamb, finding a spare inch or two, added a few words before he sealed it:

'Dear Miss Hutchinson,' he wrote: 'I subscribe most willingly to all my sister says of her Enjoyment at Cambridge. She was in silent raptures all the while *there*, and came home riding thro' the air (her 1st long outside journey), triumphing as if she had been *graduated*. I remember one foolish-pretty expression she made use of, "Bless the little churches, how pretty they are!" as those symbols of civilized life opened upon her view one after the other on this side Cambridge. You cannot proceed a mile without starting a steeple, with its little patch of villagery round it, enverduring the waste.'

According to a recently discovered letter to Talfourd, the Lambs seem to have been in Cambridge in the summer of 1819. It runs thus:

Dear T., We are at Mr. Bays's, Hatter, Trumpington Street, Cambridge. Can you come down? You will be with us, all but Bed, which you can get at an Inn. We shall be most glad to see you. Be so good as send me Hazlitt's volume, just published at Hone's, directed as above. Or, much better, bring it.

Yours, hic et ubique,

C. LAMB

The note is undated, but as it was in 1819 that William Hone published Hazlitt's *Political Essays with Sketches of Public Characters* we may assume that that was the year; while August may be deduced from two circumstances: one that the Lambs took their holidays then, and the other that in the *Examiner* for August 29 and 30, 1819, appeared a sonnet by Lamb entitled 'Written at Cambridge', and dated August 15, 1819. It begins thus:

I was not train'd in Academic bowers,
And to those learned streams I nothing owe
Which copious from those twin fair founts do flow;
Mine have been any thing but studious hours.

Yet can I fancy, wandering 'mid thy towers,
Myself a nurseling, Granta, of thy lap;
My brow seems tightening with the Doctor's cap,
And I walk *gownèd*; feel unusual powers.

Mr. Bays, by the way, lived at 11, King's Parade, Trumpington Street, which is now one of a block of three houses with rooms for undergraduates; so that this gives us yet another authentic Elian abode.

So far all has been plain sailing: when Lamb has said Cambridge he has meant Cambridge. But in 1820, by which time he had taken on the personality of Elia, he was beginning to be mysterious. In that year, staying this time again in Trumpington Street, but not for certain at Mr. Bays's, he wrote the essay called 'Oxford in the Vacation', dating it August 5, 1820, from his rooms 'facing the Bodleian', and stating how he met, in a nook at Oriel, George Dyer, who, as a matter of fact, was then engaged on his work on Cambridge privileges, and was practically chained to Cambridge libraries; and stating also, in the *London Magazine* version, how he had seen the Milton MS. in the Trinity Library, and did not like it! Why Lamb should have affected to be at Oxford and not at Cambridge, only he could explain.

To the best of my knowledge he was at

Oxford only twice in his life—once in 1800, with Gutch, and once in 1809, with Hazlitt. Hazlitt, it is worth noting, remarks on the fact (in the essay 'On the Conversation of Authors') that among Oxford's courts and colleges Lamb seemed to 'walk gownèd'—quoting from the Cambridge sonnet.

It was on the very eventful visit to Cambridge in July and August 1820, when Lamb and his sister were there for a month, that they met the little girl named Emma Isola, who was destined, as their adopted daughter, to bring into their house so much brightness and pleasure. The Lambs stayed with or near a Mrs. Paris, a sister of their London friend, Ayrton, in Trumpington Street. Living either there, or at Mrs. Watford's, a house which they visited, was this attractive child; the brother and sister took an instant liking to her; the following January—1821—Emma was their guest in London, at Great Russell Street; and after her father's death in 1823 she passed into the charge of her new friends and remained with them, when not at school or teaching, until she became the wife of Edward Moxon, the publisher and Lamb's protégé, in 1833, and left their home, on which the shadows were gathering so fast, for ever.

Emma Isola's father was Charles Isola, of Emmanuel, an Esquire Bedell of the University; her grandfather was Agostino Isola, an Italian tutor at Cambridge, among whose pupils was Wordsworth.

If we are to be chronological I must now mention one other Cambridge association bewilderingly tacked on to Oxford by its capricious chronicler. In the *London Magazine* for December 1822 appeared an amusing character sketch by Lamb entitled 'The Gentle Giantess', a farcical description of the Widow Blackett, an immensely corpulent lady, who was wont to sit in her cellar in the dog days, or amid draughts which gave her friends neuralgia, and who took the air in the evenings in Magdalen Grove. In writing to Dorothy Wordsworth in 1821, when she was staying at Trinity Lodge, with her uncle, Christopher Wordsworth, Lamb says:

Ask anybody you meet, who is the biggest woman in Cambridge and I'll hold you a wager they'll say Mrs. Smith. She broke down two benches in Trinity Gardens, one on the confines of St. John's, which occasioned a litigation between the societies as to repairing it. In warm weather she retires into an ice-cellar (literally!), and dates the returns of the years from a hot Thursday some twenty years back. She sits in a room with opposite doors and windows, to let in a thorough draught, which gives her slenderer friends tooth-aches.

That Lamb met Mrs. Smith at Cambridge in 1820 we know, because Crabb Robinson, who was on circuit here at the time, joined them in a rubber. But what a man to edit!

And there Lamb's association with Cambridge ends, unless we count his intimacy with William Frend and his daughter Sophie Frend (afterwards Mrs. Augustus De Morgan and mother of the author of *Joseph Vance*) as another bond.

After so much minutiae and confusion the time has perhaps come to recapitulate. Briefly, then, we find that Lamb probably first visited Cambridge previous to the end of 1794, when Coleridge left. His next visit was to Manning in 1801. His next with his sister in Hell-Fire Dick's coach in 1815. His next the sojourn of August 1819, providing the Cambridge sonnet. And then the visit of a month in July and August 1820, leading to the essay whimsically transferred to Oxford, and to the account of Mrs. Smith, of Cambridge, as Oxford's Widow Blackett; and leading also to the adoption of Emma Isola.

Both therefore in Lamb's work and life Cambridge may be said to have no little share; and although it gave him Manning's stimulating intellectual heartiness at a time when he needed it, Cambridge is, I think, most to be felicitated with for providing for his many lonely hours after his retirement from the India House that merry and sensible girl who was to be so valuable a companion and a friend—that 'girl of gold', as he called her, that 'silent brown girl': silent, and yet at the same time, as he said, the 'best female talker' he had ever known.

It was with mixed feelings that Lamb gave his consent for her marriage to Edward Moxon in 1833. Mary Lamb's attacks were becoming more frequent and acute; his own health was failing; his home was, he knew only too well, no place for a girl on the threshold of life. A few months after the wedding he wrote a letter to both husband and wife, which seems to me not the least courageous effort of a noble and courageous life. It begins with criticism—for Moxon had the sonnet habit very badly—and incidentally Lamb urges him to quarrel with his wife whenever he can, for she is 'beautiful in reconciliation'. And then he describes how he has been lured once again into an excess of

78

conviviality, such as Emma had so often—and I feel, so understandingly—deplored. He adds:

> 'Tell it not in Gath, Emma, lest the daughters triumph!' I am at the end of my tether. I wish you would come on Tuesday with your fair bride. Why can't you. Do . . . Come and bring a sonnet on Mary's birthday. Love to the whole Moxonry, and tell E. I every day love her more, and miss her less.

Miss her less! Never, if truth is to be told, did he miss her more or need her more. It was another of those white lies which Cambridge fostered in him; another absolute inversion of the fact; Oxford for Cambridge once again: but what a fine brave tragic falsehood!

1910

HELL-FIRE DICK

I HAVE before said that the time is never quite ripe to edit Lamb; and another proof of that statement occurred last evening when I brought home the Rev. J. Richardson's *Recollections of the Last Half Century* (1856) and came upon Mr. Richard Vaughan. For it was several years earlier that I had been in need of that gentleman and could not then find him.

Writing to Sarah Hutchinson in August 1815, Mary Lamb, in what is perhaps her most charming letter, of which I have just quoted a large portion, describes a visit just paid by herself and her brother to Cambridge. 'We set off on the outside of the Cambridge coach from Fetter Lane at eight o'clock and were driven into Cambridge in great triumph by Hell-Fire Dick five minutes before three.' To these words, when preparing an edition of the letters, I could put no illuminating commentary; but now I know Dick well.

Richard Vaughan, or Hell-Fire Dick, after losing his licence as the landlord of the Bell at Cambridge, owing to the effects of his popularity among the undergraduates, returned to driving and tooled the up 'Telegraph' from the Sun in Trumpington Street half-way to London, and brought the down 'Telegraph' back every afternoon. He was a very horsey-looking man, 'bony, gaunt, and grim', and his complexion was 'indicative of continual exposure to the winds and the weather and to habitual indulgence in what is taken to keep the weather out'. He possessed a rough and ready wit which found its way into the world from the box of the 'Telegraph' by the medium of a voice which a boatswain in a storm would envy, and when not on duty he was a sportsman of varied interests, of which cock-fighting was chief; and he instructed the young bloods in driving.

Such was the coachman who deposited Charles and Mary Lamb in Cambridge in August 1815.

1913

MEN OF WEIGHT

NOW and again it has been suggested by some sanguine innovator—a poet with the backward look or an architect not so over-burdened with commissions as yet to be mercenary—that the sign-board shall be revived in London. Although belonging to neither of these groups, I am as strongly in favour of it; for the sign can be a very attractive thing, gay or grave in colour and simple or fantastic in design, and a hundred of them hanging out from their bars at odd altitudes would make our streets amusing and picturesque. Trade also should follow this form of flag. But the reform tarries or is left to tea shops and such little odd concerns as flourish (or not) in single rooms in South Moulton Street, where there are more signs, for its length, than, I believe, in any London thoroughfare.

Were the board to come back, one of the pleasantest old world signs would be that of the 'Coffee Mill', which would be seen merrily flaunting itself a few yards from the foot of St. James's Street on the left as you descend the

hill; for it is the original style of that ancient
wine office at No. 3 which you may have
noticed even if you never have entered it: a
dark sombre house of business, externally,
with a side front on the little backwater known
as Pickering Place, which still defies the march
of progress but has not recaptured its popularity either as a gaming centre, as it was in
the eighteenth century, when it was called
Pickering Court, or as a duelling ground.

Pickering Place owes its name to the worthy
tea and tobacco merchant who was its principal
resident, and it was his business—at the sign of
the 'Coffee Mill'—which came in time into
the hands of the present occupiers of No. 3
St. James's Street, Messrs. Berry Brothers & Co.,
but they, relinquishing their predecessor's
versatility, pin their faith solely to the generous
juices of the grape. It is not, however, of wine
that I would write, but of avoirdupois. Men of
weight.

Surprising things happen in London so
often that gradually the element of surprise
disappears, and it is only a question of time for
us to be prepared for all. A recent metropolitan
discovery of mine—which I might have made
thirty years before, if the clock had struck—
is that at the sign of the 'Coffee Mill' in St.

James's Street is a pair of scales on which, for fully a century and a half, all that was most eminent in human form has sat to be weighed, and is still sitting; and that ever since the year 1765 accurate records of illustrious and often regal ponderosity have been kept. It was absurd to have lived in London since 1892 and to have learned this only in 1920; but that illustrates both the tangle of caprice which (for want of a better word) we call life, and the inexhaustibility of our city.

'If you want to know how much Charles Lamb weighed in 1814, I can tell you the way to find out'—it was that casual remark which put me at last on the scent; and now I can supply devout Elians with the information that in 1814, when he was thirty-nine, their divinity turned the scale, in his boots, at 9 stone 3 lb.; or almost a stone more than I was expecting after so much evidence as to his 'immaterial' form. But his boots may have been very heavy. And also, I am bound to add, it may have been another Charles Lamb. The name is not uncommon: a Brighton alderman in my extreme youth bore it and bore with it an inflamed nose of majestic proportion; and an Enfield butcher had the hardihood to call himself Charles Lamb too.

Having made the start I continued investigations, with the assistance of an analysis of the book which one of the partners had made. Keeping to literature I discovered that Lord Byron, whom we know to have been sensitive about his bulk, was weighed many times, first in 1806, when he was living at No. 8, only five doors away. He was then 13 stone 12 lb. in his boots. This result must have distressed exceedingly one who lived in fear of embonpoint, even to the drinking of vinegar and general mortification of the flesh. In 1807, in shoes only, he had got it down to 10 stone 13 lb., and in 1811, again in shoes, to 9 stone 11½ lb. Tom Moore, his Lordship's biographer, seems similarly to have decreased, for in 1807 he was 10 stone 6 lb. and in 1809, 8 stone 13 lb. Another famous man who can also have had no wish to lose his figure, and who will go down to history as much for his insolent question as to the identity of the Prince Regent (with whom he had quarrelled) 'Who's your fat friend?' as for his fastidiousness in ties, dwindled too. In 1798 he was 12 stone 4 lb., in boots; in 1811, 13 stone 10 lb. in boots and frock; and in 1815, 12 stone 10½ lb., in shoes. In 1815 Brummell's reign was ending, for a year later he had to fly from his creditors

to Calais. None the less there is still one more
entry, in 1822, suggesting that he was able to
visit the scenes of his old triumphs yet once
again, and then he was 10 stone 13 lb. in boots.

As for the fat friend, he was here many
times. In 1791 he weighed 17 stone 4 lb., in
boots; in 1798 16 stone 'after gout'; in 1800,
17 stone 9 lb. in hat and boots; and later that
year, 16 stone 5 lb. 'after gout'; in 1803,
'with gout', 15 stone 8 lb.

Many of William Hickey's boon companions
came to the 'Coffee Mill' to be weighed, but
there is no record of a visit by himself. The
Earl of Peterborough, for example, who was
one of the original members of the Dining
Club of twenty—'the dinner to consist of every
article procurable whether in or out of season':
a good preparation for the 'Coffee Mill's'
scales. Thomas Creevey the diarist was on the
heavy side: in 1808, 14 stone, and in 1837,
15 stone 7 lb. Abraham Hayward was much
lighter, being, in 1836, in boots, only 8 stone
2½ lb. Joseph Hume, the economist and Radi-
cal, before he was weighed laid aside his coat
and his watch but retained his boots, while
quite a number of the more particular clients
stripped absolutely and had the doors closed,
among them Lord Dunmore. Charles James

Fox in 1773, in his boots, weighed 12 stone 8 lb.; in 1781, in shoes, 13 stone 12 lb. George Cruikshank was on the scales in 1826, but how the author of *The Bottle* and *The Triumph of Bacchus* could bring himself to enter this establishment I cannot understand. Many illustrious soldiers are in the records, among them Sir John Moore, 12 stone 1 lb. in shoes in 1784, and 11 stone 11½ lb. in half boots in 1808; Sir Colin Campbell, 11 stone 6 lb. in 1827; and Captain Fred Burnaby, who was a giant, 14 stone 10½ lb. The Iron Duke is absent.

The heaviest man who ever burdened the 'Coffee Mill' scales was Mr. George Drummond who, in 1850, registered 25 stone 12 lb. But his was negligible bulk compared with that of Mr. Bright of Maldon, who, at the age of twenty-nine, when he laid aside his panoply, weighed 44 stone. No visit of Mr. Bright to the 'Coffee Mill' is recorded, but there is a print on the office wall depicting the wager between Mr. Codd and Mr. Hants, the bet being that seven men could be buttoned within Mr. Bright's waistcoat. It was easily won, on December 1, 1750, in the 'Black Bull' at Maldon, kept at that time by the Widow Day. Whether there are any such colossi now I cannot say. Mr. Chesterton is, to the familiar press, the recognized example of heroic girth, and many are the jokes on the subject—such as his gallantry in standing in an omnibus to offer his seat to three ladies—but there is an element of myth in the whole affair. It is my privilege to know Mr. Chesterton, and I can assure those who do not that he is not so immense as all that—not, I mean, in body. In mind and sympathies, yes. Meanwhile, just to prove that an interest in amplitude and pinguidity still obtains, let me mention that I saw a Scotch paper the other day in which the proprietor of a Wax-works Exhibition advertised for a charwoman:'Must weigh over 20 stone. Wages £1 a day.'

1922

LAMB AS AN ORATOR

FEW hobbies are more attractive to me than the preparation of books for private circulation only; and I wish I had more time to give to it. Perhaps it will be a solace of old age. Meanwhile, I can admire the efforts of others, and seldom have I admired anything more than the volume entitled *The Records of the Amicable Society of Blues*, compiled by the late H. A. Roberts, who was himself an Amicable Blue of high distinction. It is not only a very human document, but a piece of beautiful typography.

And more than that, it probably clears up for ever an event of importance that for too many years has been wrapt in mystery: it tells us at what dinner Charles Lamb was the guest of honour when his speech in reply to the toast of the evening could get no farther than the one word 'Gentlemen'. We knew about this festive evening from a very lengthy letter from Lamb to Mrs. William Wordsworth (written at the East India House, on East India House paper, and in East India

House time), in which he has something to say about public speaking. 'Lectures', he says, with reference to a course that Coleridge was giving on Shakespeare and Poetical Literature, in a hall in Fleur de Luce Court, Fetter Lane, 'are not much to my taste, whatever the lecturer may be. If *read*, they are dismal, flat, and you can't think why you are brought together to hear a man read his works which you could read so much better at leisure yourself; if delivered extempore, I am always in pain lest the gift of utterance should suddenly fail the orator in the middle, as it did me at the dinner given in honour of me at the London Tavern. "Gentlemen", said I, and there I stoppt—the rest my feelings were under the necessity of supplying.'

Now, none of Lamb's editors, however meritorious and diligent, have been able to place that historic harangue. Not one of us. But I think that Mr. Roberts has done so; for his work is the record of a club of old scholars of Christ's Hospital, and by consulting the minute books he discovered some very pertinent entries bearing upon the great secret, certain of which are reproduced in his pages in unimpeachable facsimile. First, that at the dinner of the Amicable Blues on January 14,

1817, 'a work by C. Lamb on Christ's Hospital was read', and was followed by the resolution to invite C. Lamb to dine at the ensuing meeting. (Why C. Lamb was not himself an Amicable Blue is an enigma; but let that pass.) This work of C. Lamb on Christ's Hospital, his old school, is not the *Elia* essay, but the 'Recollections of Christ's Hospital', first published in the *Gentleman's Magazine* in 1813; and a second enigma is why it had taken the Amicable Blues so long to hear of it. Let that pass too: people can be woefully behind the times in the matter of good literature. There seems then to have followed a correspondence between C. Lamb and Henry Woodthorpe, junior, the president for the year, with the result that on February 11, 1817, at five o'clock, C. Lamb sat down to dine with the Amicable Blues as their special guest.

The scene was the famous London Tavern, in Bishopsgate, where the heads of the East India House (at which C. Lamb carried on his long private correspondences) were wont to entertain nabobs and other distinguished guests. Present were Henry Woodthorpe, senior, chairman, Messrs. Sparks, Nixson, Hill, Jackson, Deane, Few, Pinhey, Hewitt, Steel, Brown, Blenkinsopp, and Williams, secretary. There

were two visitors: C. Lamb and Mr. Charles
Cole. Number in all, fifteen. The correspondence between C. Lamb and the president was
read, and we may be sure it was worth hearing.
(Are there no Woodthorpe descendants who
can produce the originals?) And then I suppose
came the immortal speech; and who would
have cavilled at its brevity?—for to be called
gentlemen unqualified by such a judge is
praise enough. C. Lamb, had he been so
mechanical as to have gone on, might have
told the company that on the preceding day
he had reached the age of forty-two.

There is still no absolute proof that this was
the dinner to which he referred in his letter
to Mrs. Wordsworth, but the presumptive
evidence is overwhelming. It was given in
his honour, it was given at the London Tavern,
and it was given only a year before his letter,
which is dated February 18, 1818. 'The' dinner,
he calls it; not a dinner.

For Lamb's only other post-prandial speech
of which we have any record we must turn to
an undated letter to Mrs. Wordsworth's sister
—or rather postscript to one of Mary Lamb's
—where he says, 'Apropos of birds—the other
day, at a large dinner, being call'd upon
for a toast, I gave, as the best toast I knew,

"Woodcock toast," which was drunk with 3 cheers.'

I shall continue to think of Lamb as the hero of Mr. Roberts's book, even though others may set Richard Thornton in that high place; and if they do I shall have no real quarrel with them. Richard Thornton, whose coloured portrait by Dighton serves as frontispiece, was the famous merchant and underwriter of Lloyd's, known in the City as the 'Duke of Dantzig', and later as 'Old Dicky', who was president of the Amicable Blues in 1838. A year younger than Lamb, he had almost as different a career as could be imagined. This adventurous financier was a remarkable friend to England as well as to other countries in times of stress. Hemp being badly needed during the Napoleonic wars, he himself fitted out a vessel and sailed her to Memel for a cargo of it, fighting a naval engagement on his way. His brother, whom he left behind in Memel, was able to give early news of Napoleon's retreat from Moscow, thus enabling the 'Duke of Dantzig' to net £200,000. Both Spain and Portugal were on occasion financed by Thornton. He was an owner of racehorses, but, as speed is not all, he was accustomed to bet heavily on a favourite cheesemite at the lunch-table. His passion for wagers led to some amusing episodes at Lloyd's, and he was the first to insure against the risk of Queen Victoria having twins at her first confinement. 'Twins, indeed,' says Mr. Roberts, 'were an obsession with him, for old men alive to-day will remember him standing with his back to the fire at Lloyd's offering to bet all young newly married members one hundred to one against the double event.' His last words have a fine ring: 'Stand aside, please,' he said to those around his bed—he was nearly ninety —'let me see the sun go down; I shall never see him rise again.' It recalls Goethe's 'More light!' and probably Goethe and Thornton were even wider apart than Thornton and Lamb. Hard for such men as 'Old Dicky' to die, especially when they are leaving nearly three million pounds!

1925

MRS. CONRADY

A T a time when more than the usual attention is being paid to Charles Lamb it
may be proper to repeat an old question,
'Who was Mrs. Conrady?' This lady's face,
it will be remembered, is the subject of a
minute analysis in the *Last Essays of Elia*.
I quote a little from Lamb's generous tribute:
'. . . It is not as if some Apelles had picked
out here a lip—and there a chin—out of the
collected ugliness of Greece, to frame a model
by. It is a symmetrical whole. We challenge
the minutest connoisseur to cavil at any part
or parcel of the countenance in question;
to say that this, or that, is improperly placed.
We are convinced that true ugliness, no less
than is affirmed of true beauty, is the result of
harmony. . . . The first time that you are
indulged with a sight of her face is an era in
your existence ever after. You are glad to
have seen it—like Stonehenge.'

Lamb, so often an innovator, here again is
a pioneer. After centuries in which poets and

lovers were extolling feminine beauty, we have a new kind of writing: the careful and discriminating eulogy of feminine plainness, done so tenderly as never to make us wince at any fault in taste.

It is the treatment that makes the novelty, for whenever hitherto, at any rate in my reading, ugly women had been referred to, it was in the coarsest way and very quickly, without elaboration, as in translations from Martial, in Herrick's epigrams, in Swift, and other eighteenth-century satirists. The old *Spectator*, while finding much scope for its wit and fancy in ugliness in men, a perennially popular theme, allowed that women could be ugly too, but in enunciating the heresy hid behind a female correspondent—Hecatissa—who in the number for April 25, 1711, flaunts her want of grace. The *Spectator*, indeed, if all men were comely, would have been hard put to it to fill some of its pages. As early as the seventeenth number, March 20, 1711, Steele was creating the Ugly Club.

This particular kind of humour is no longer current. To-day we take more for granted and are prompt in our dismissal of the Gothic in the faces of others. 'No oil painting,' we say, and pass on; although oil-paintings are not what they were.

It would indeed be amusing if a new Mrs. Conrady were to arise and rain influence. She would have to-day, in our photographic era, an opportunity such as she could not hope for then. In the eighteen-twenties, when Lamb was extolling the original one, there were few opportunities for people at large to know what she was like. They could see in one of the London picture galleries her portrait —supposing any artist to have dared first to risk his reputation by painting her and then to risk it again by exhibiting the result. They could see in the print-shop windows reproductions of it—again supposing that any engraver had the initiative and courage. But that is all; for such few illustrations as got into the newspapers were those of malefactors who were wanted by the police. Thus the derivative Fair, always so quick to imitate the cast of features of their dominant sisters, had no chance to follow and popularise the Conrady type. How they perform so swiftly and completely these feats of mimicry, Heaven alone can tell; but the fact remains that they can. The model has but to be sufficiently admired for the copies to multiply. How this year the girls can have longer noses than they had last, and how next year those organs may shorten again—these are profound mysteries. Finding them at the moment all so much alike, I, personally, would give a welcome to an infusion of the Conrady individuality.

But who was Mrs. Conrady? One would not expect to find the answer in Mr. Blunden's exquisitely understanding book, *Charles Lamb and His Contemporaries*, recently published, because Mr. Blunden is concerned with higher and deeper things; but some of the many explorers into Lamb's life who, I am sure, are now at work, will, I hope, solve the problem. Mrs. Conrady may, of course, have been an imaginary woman invented for the purpose of the work in hand; but I doubt this. Invention was not Lamb's line. He may often have superimposed upon truth his own 'matter-of-lies', but there was a solid foundation of truth beneath. All his fantastic people have a substratum of fact. Ralph Bigod, of the *Essays*, the borrower, was in real life John Fenwick; James Elia of the *Essays*, the collector, was in real life John Lamb; 'Tom Pry's Wife', the inquisitive woman, was Mrs. Godwin; Mrs. Battle, the whist tyrant, was Mrs. Burney;

the 'Gentle Giantess' was Mrs. Smith of Cambridge; and so forth. The only characters of whose names in real life we know nothing are Captain Jackson, the exaggerator; Juke Judkins, the miser; and Mrs. Conrady.

1933

LAMB AND THE MEASLES

THE actual text of a letter from Charles Lamb to his friends at St. Valery-sur-Somme, James Kenney and his wife, in 1816—printed in my own edition of Lamb's letters not too accurately, and dated 1817—has led me to inquire further not only into the relations of Elia with the fair land of France but into the life story of the 'child wife' he met there: Louisa Holcroft, James Kenney's step-daughter.

To begin with, let me say that although European struggles had never claimed much of his attention, Lamb was pro-Napoleon. Not long after Waterloo, to which his correspondence makes no reference, he wrote to Southey: 'After all, Bonaparte is a fine fellow, as my barber says, and I should not mind standing bare-headed at his table to do him service in his fall. They should have given him Hampton Court or Kensington, with a tether extending forty miles round London. Qu. would not the people have ejected the Bruns-wicks some day in his favour?' That was in

1815. A year later, in the letter to his friends, the Kenneys, to 'Saint Wallery sure some', he finishes with the pious wish, 'Vive la beau France et revive ma cher Empreur!' The critical and decisive battle near Brussels in June, 1815, received, however, no notice in his correspondence, nor had he had anything to say, ten years earlier, of Trafalgar, although when Nelson died, he remarked, in a letter to Hazlitt, 'I have followed him in Fancy since I saw him walking in Pall Mall (I was prejudiced against him before) looking just as a Hero should look.'

The letter to the Kenneys to which I refer is dated from 'Lonres', but whether Lamb's French was as bad as he makes it, out of sheer devilment, or because the Christ's Hospital curriculum had ignored the language, I have no notion, although his spelling of the austere Chateaubriand as Chatty Briant was, I am certain, a perversion as wilful as it is delightful.

The 1816 letter says nothing about a project for any visit to France, but it has this passage on the inhabitants of that country: 'Lord, what things you see that travel. I dare say the people are all French wherever you go. What an overwhelming effect that must have! I have stood one of 'em at a time, but two I generally found overwhelming. I used to cut and run; but in their own vineyards maybe they are endurable enough. They say marmosets in Senegambia are as pleasant as the day's long, jumping and chattering in the orange twigs, but transport 'em one by one over here into England, they turn into monkeys, some with tails, some without, and are obliged to be kept in cages.' In spite of this far from gallant estimate of our neighbours across the Channel, Lamb was willing to suppress his fears and actually be among them; and in 1822 he and his sister and his sister's nurse set sail from Brighton to Dieppe. Miss Lamb, having one of her attacks, had to stay at Amiens until she was well; Lamb went on alone, dividing his time between the Kenneys, then at Versailles, and the Hôtel de l'Europe near the Palais Royal. Having to return to England before his sister had arrived, he left a note advising her that the best of Paris was 'the Borough side of the Seine'.

Lamb's own pleasure in the gay city was considerably increased by a mistake made by a waiter on the first morning after his arrival, when, being, like all Englishmen after the French breakfast, hungry at about eleven, he entered a café and ordered an egg, probably saying briefly 'un œuf, vite,' which might be construed into 'eau de vie'. Anyway, instead of an egg the waiter brought a glass of brandy: a confusion which so enchanted Lamb that during the rest of his visit he was continually ordering eggs.

His hosts at Versailles were James Kenney, the dramatist, and his wife, a Frenchwoman, the widow of Thomas Holcroft, another dramatist. There were also in the house Holcroft's children, Fanny and Louisa (the 'child-wife') and Tom, and Kenney's children: the youngest of them, Charles Lamb Kenney, born in 1821, who in his time was to become a dramatist too, being Elia's god-son. Also in Paris were John Poole, author of *Paul Pry*, and John Howard Payne, another playwright and the author of the words to 'Home, Sweet Home', and in Payne's company Lamb met Talma, the tragedian (who could speak English, having once been a dentist in London), and saw his portrait of Shakespeare on a pair of bellows and believed in it—but that is another story.

References to Paris in Lamb's letters after his return prove that he enjoyed his time there. Both to John Clare and to Barron Field he is ecstatic about frogs as a delicacy:

The nicest little rabbity things you ever tasted. Do look about for them. Make Mrs. Clare pick off the hind quarters, boil them plain with parsley and butter. The fore quarters are not so good. She may let them hop off by themselves.

And again:

Imagine a Lilliputian rabbit! They fricassee them; but, in my mind, drest, seethed, plain, with parsley and butter would have been the decision of Apicius. . . . Paris is a glorious picturesque old city. London looks mean and new to it, as the town of Washington would, seen after *it*. But they have no St. Paul's or Westminster Abbey. The Seine, so much despised by Cockneys, is exactly the size to run thro' a magnificent street; palaces a mile long on one side, lofty Edinbro' stone (O the glorious antiques!); houses on the other. The Thames disunites London and Southwark.

Again, to John Howard Payne:

Paris, which I hardly knew whether I like when I was in it, is an object of no small magnitude with me now. I want to be going to the Jardin des Plantes (is that right, Louisa?) with you—to Pere de la Chaise, La Morgue, and all the sentimentalities. . . . N.B.—My friend White knows Paris thoroughly, and does not want a guide. We did, and had one. We both join in thanks. Do you remember a Blue-Silk Girl (English) at the Luxembourg, that did not much seem to attend to the

Pictures, who fell in love with you, and whom I fell in love with—an inquisitive, prying, curious Beauty—where is she?

This letter is signed 'Votre Tres Humble Serviteur, Charlois Agneau, *alias* C. Lamb'. In another letter to Payne, Monsieur Agneau says:

> I am sensible of the want of method in this letter, but I have been deprived of the connecting organ, by a practice I have fallen into since I left Paris, of taking too much strong spirits of a night. I must return to the Hôtel de l'Europe and Macon.

Lamb came home first, Mary Lamb following in the care of Henry Crabb Robinson. Writing to Mrs. Kenney on September 11, 1822, Lamb says of his sister's experiences at the Custom House:

> She did not succeed in saving Robinson's fine waistcoat. They could not comprehend how a waistcoat, marked Henry Robinson, could be a part of Miss Lamb's wearing apparel. So they seized it for the king, who will probably appear in it at the next levee.

He adds a little note for Sophy, Louisa's twin:

> You and she are my better half, a quarter apiece. She and you are my pretty sixpence— you the head and she the tail. Sure, Heaven that made you so alike must pardon the error of an inconsiderate moment, should I for love of you,

love her too well. Do you think laws were made
for lovers? I think not.

Had it not been for 'the tail of the sixpence',
we should not have one of Lamb's most
attractive pieces of nonsense—his letter about
measles, the letter indeed to which all these
remarks have been preliminary.[1] Louisa Holcroft, not long before her marriage to Badams,
was staying, in December 1828, with her
step-parents, the Kenneys, at 12 Brunswick
Square, where measles were prevailing. After
a few lines embodying a message from his
sister, Lamb continues:

> You will see by my altered scrawl, that I am
> not so well this morning. I got up with a fever'd
> skin and spots are come out all over me. Pray God
> it is not the measles. You did not let any of the
> children touch the seal with their little measly
> hands, did you? You should be careful when
> contagion is in the house.
>
> Pray God, your letter may not have convey'd
> the disorder! Our poor Postman looks flush'd
> since. What a thing it would be to introduce disease
> into a whole village. Yet so simple a thing as a
> Letter has been known to convey a malady.
> I look at your note. I see it is wafer'd, not sealed.

[1] The original is in the Henry E. Huntington collection in
America and it is quoted here from Ainger's edition of Lamb's
Works by permission of Messrs. Macmillan.

That makes it more likely. Wafers are flour, and I've known a serious illness to be communicated in a piece of plumb cake. I never had the measles. How my head throbs! You cannot be too cautious, dear Louisa, what you do under such circum——

I am a little better than when I broke off at the last word. Your good sense will point out to you that the deficient syllables should be stances. Circumstances. If I am incoherent, impute it to alarm. I will walk in the air——

I am not much refresh'd. The air seem'd hot and muggy. Some how I feel quite irritable——there is no word in English—a la la varole—we have no phrase to answer it—smallpoxical comes the nearest. May be 'twas worse than the measles what Charles has. I will send for Dr. Asbury.

I have seen the apothecary. He pronounces my complaint to be, as I feared, of the variola kind, but gives me hopes I shall not be much marked. I hope we shall all get well together. But at my time of life it is attended with more hazards. Whatever becomes of me, I shall leave the world without a harsh thought of you. It was only a girlish imprudence. I am quite faint. Two pimples more came out within this last minute. Mary is crying. She looks red. So does Becky. I must go to bed.

Yours in constant Pain

C L

You will see by my Will, if it comes to that—I bear you no ill w—— Oh!

—That is good fun, is it not? And a kind of fun which, although plenty of people have tried their hands at it since, was not common in 1828. Sydney Smith was a master at it, and we find it a little later in the letters of Edward Lear. But Lamb, who came before so many writers, not always essayists, was again an innovator.

It was not, however, for Lamb, the unmarrying, that Louisa was intended, but for John Badams, the chemist, a friend of Thomas Carlyle. As it chanced, the young people settled at Enfield, near the Lambs, and it is to this circumstance that we owe one of the most melancholy examples of prejudice and warped judgment in the language. For it was on a visit to the Badams in 1831, and under the very roof of the child-wife, that Lamb was seen by Carlyle under such disadvantageous circumstances, and was thus described: 'A more pitiful, ricketty, gasping, staggering, stammering Tomfool I do not know . . . Poor England, when such a despicable abhorrence is named genius.'

When Swinburne, always passionately eager to condemn or to extol, came upon this passage in Carlyle's *Reminiscences*, his mind could not be tranquillized until he had composed two

sonnets of protest, of which the second runs
thus:

Sweet heart, forgive me for thine own sweet sake,
　　Whose kind blithe soul such seas of sorrow swam,
　　And for my love's sake, powerless as I am
For love to praise thee, or like thee to make
Music of mirth where hearts less pure would break,
　　Less pure than thine, our life-unspotted Lamb.
　　Things hatefullest thou hadst not heart to damn,
Nor wouldst have set thine heel on this dead snake.
Let worms consume its memory with its tongue,
The fang that stabbed fair Truth, the lip that stung
　　Men's memories uncorroded with its breath.
Forgive me, that with bitter words like his
I mix the gentlest English name that is,
　　The tenderest held of all that know not death.

It is only fair to add (as I am told by a
kinsman of the poet) that when Carlyle was
asked to meet the author of *Atalanta in Calydon*
he replied: 'Mr. Swinburne lives in a sewer
and contributes to it, and if he comes to see me
I will tell him more.'

1933

THE MAN WITH FORTY-SEVEN
FRIENDS

WE have all seen series of mural paint-
ings representing the most noteworthy
or most illustratable deeds of one heroic
figure—such as those at Blenheim in honour
of the great Marlborough, and those in the
Louvre, by Rubens, celebrating the glories of
Marie de Medicis. But to find a room dedicated
in this way to the friends of one single man
is new; new, at any rate, to me, although the
room in question has been in existence in
London for many, many years, during two
of which I was every day only a few yards
distant and although I have a peculiar interest
in some of the portraits. So late can we come
to things!

The room is the lecture-room, once the
dining-room, of University Hall in Gordon
Street, and the man thus honoured is Henry
Crabb Robinson, Lamb's 'Old Crabb', whose
portrait is at one end, a marble bust of him
at the other, and round the walls no fewer than
forty-seven life-size and full-length repre-

sentations of his friends, English, French, and German, ranging from Charles and Mary Lamb to Arthur Hugh Clough and Mme. de Staël. I call them life-size, but I fancy they are rather above it—Lamb certainly is, if the descriptions of his frail form (I quote Charles Tween's testimony elsewhere in this book) are accurate—and not only are they all of commanding height, but all are robust and vigorous, as scholars and poets, philosophers and divines too often are not; and all appear to me of much the same age, although, of course, there were wide differences, Samuel Rogers, for instance, being at the time of painting far older than R. H. Hutton of the *Spectator*, and Goethe than James Martineau. But it was perhaps wise of the artist to choose a favourable mean of health and years and subordinate them all to it, for these frescoes are not realistic but symbolical, almost as though the theme were a company of the bland and blessed in Paradise.

As for the painter, who includes himself in the last and youngest group, it was Edward Armitage, R.A., whom I remember seeing as a very old man in his house in St. John's Wood, and who was almost my first artist, by reason of his picture of Samson struggling with the lion which used to hang high in the Brighton Museum: a building otherwise notable to me for its mosaic portrait of the First Gentleman in Europe, whose stables, now the Dome, were hard by, and, upstairs, for the clock with all its wonderful works on view and the Willett collection of historical jugs and mugs and pictorial plates. Since Armitage decorated University Hall at his own expense some years after most of the people depicted were dead, I am wondering where he got his likenesses from, for only a few of them were in time to be photographed or even daguerreotyped. Some, of course, he could himself have known, for he was born in 1817 and thus was seventeen when Lamb died, and fifty when, at the age of ninety-one, Crabb Robinson at last relinquished a world in which he was so vocal and, though exacting, happy; but for most of them Armitage would have had to work from other portraits.

It is given to few men to have forty-seven friends of any kind, and fewer to have forty-seven friends of such intellectual distinction and eminence as to be worth painting on walls; and I know of no other instance. I must give their names, just to put on record so remarkable a group and so remarkable

an achievement. But first a word on 'Old
Crabb' himself, whose manuscript diary, which
I have perused, is the principal treasure of
the Dr. Williams Library, preserved in neigh-
bouring rooms.

Robinson was the son of a tanner, and, like
Ouida, was born at Bury St. Edmunds but,
unlike her, wrote no flamboyant fiction and has
no memorial there. Beginning as a journalist,
he was one of the first foreign correspondents
of *The Times*. Afterwards he became an
advocate, and retired as soon as he had
amassed a competence, saying that the two
wisest deeds in his life were going to the Bar
and, in 1828, leaving it. His leisure thereafter
he devoted to travel, talk, amity, and good
works. But for his interest in the students of
University College, which he helped to found,
there would be no University Hall.

Crabb Robinson, though a lawyer, a collector of serious intellects, and an undefeatable
debater, could not intimidate Lamb, two of
whose most elvish letters were written to him.
Possibly the circumstance that the two men
were exact contemporaries made the association easier. The first letter in the correspondence
was dated March 12, 1808; the last to be preserved was of 1832. It was good-humouredly

to torment Robinson, when racked by rheu-
matism or lumbago, that in April, 1829, Lamb
drew up that famous list of agonies; and the
account of Randal Norris's death, which I
quote earlier in this book, was written to him.

Robinson was chosen out of all Lamb's
friends for the triumphant message on March
29, 1825: 'I have left the d . . . d India House
for Ever! Give me great joy,' and when,
in 1822, as I have related also earlier in this
book, Lamb and Miss Lamb and Miss Lamb's
attendant, Miss James, went to Paris for a
week or so, Robinson went too.

Now for the seven-and-forty just ones. They
begin, just inside the door on the left, with
Coleridge, Mary Lamb (for whose well-being,
after her brother's death, Robinson made
himself largely responsible), Charles Lamb,
Southey, Wordsworth (depicted as too old,
with white whiskers), William Blake (whom
Robinson never tired of extolling, and whom
Lamb, who also admired him, mistakenly
called Robert), and Flaxman the sculptor,
many of whose works, in the Flaxman Gallery
at University College, were Robinson's gift.
The corresponding group on the other side of
the door is German, comprising Von Knebb,
Tieck, Goethe, Arndt, Schiller, Herder, and

MARY AND CHARLES LAMB
From the Fresco by Edward Armitage, R.A., in University Hall, London
Reproduced by kind permission of Dr. Williams's Library

Wieland. Before Carlyle and after William
Taylor of Norwich, it was Crabb Robinson
who did more than any Englishman to intro-
duce the German thinkers and poets to this
country's attention.

Now for some more Englishmen: William
Hazlitt, very like a parson; William Godwin,
in a cape; Thomas Clarkson, W. S. Landor,
and Gilbert Wakefield, present among whom
is Mrs. Barbauld, one of the trinity that Lamb
called the three bald women, the others being
Mrs. Inchbald and Mrs. Baldwin, the name
taken by Mrs. Godwin when she published
Lamb's books for children.

The only other female intellects represented
in the room are Lady Byron, who, though
surrounded by a very mixed assemblage of
what now would be called highbrows, does not
seem in the least overawed, Mme. de Staël
and the Duchess Amalia, who are found in a
group completed by Schlegel and Savigny.
Lady Byron's associates comprise Edward
Irving, the galvanic preacher, whose Catholic
Apostolic church is only a few yards away, in
Gordon Square; Samuel Rogers, the banker-
poet or poet-banker (no, banker-poet); Edward Quillinan, the friend of Wordsworth,
whose name Lamb couldn't spell; Lord Cran-

worth, the judge; Sir T. N. Talfourd, the biographer of Lamb; the Rev. F. W. Robertson 'of Brighton'; Dr. Arnold, head master of Rugby; Ambrose Poynter, the architect; and the Chevalier Bunsen. Finally, there are a number of publicists and divines, the kind of men that old Crabb would have been serious with, of several of whom I have no knowledge: the Rev. P. Le Breton, James Haywood, J. P. Heywood, J. Thorneley, E. W. Field, W. S. Cookson, James Martineau, W. B. Carpenter, A. H. Clough, the poet, R. H. Hutton, J. L. Taylor, E. Beesly, and, No. 47, Armitage, the painter, shyly escaping to a corner.

And why were they painted round the walls of this room? As a proof that 'a catholic spirit alone can secure to itself the love and attachment of great and good men of widely different opinions'. Furthermore, in the hope that this memorial may incite in those who visit it a life-ambition for similar attachments, 'such as can be based only on a reverence for the freedom of individual thought and not on the coincidences of doubtful speculation'. I wonder who wrote those words. They sound very Crabb-like.

1932

LETTERS TO MARTIN BURNEY

MR. INGLESIDE, who could not be diverted from the cabinet containing the autographs, suddenly exclaimed, "Why you old fox, if you haven't some letters from Lamb to Martin Burney! I thought they had all disappeared.'

'So they had,' said the doctor, smiling the masterful smile of the successful collector: 'but only into that drawer! But I have very few. Where the others are is truly a mystery. In America very likely. Read them to us, Ingleside. They will probably be as fresh to me as to any of you, for it's years since I bought them. I remember annotating them at the time.'

Mr. Ingleside arranged them in chronological order. 'This,' he said, 'according to your note, Staminer, is the earliest. It is undated, and conjecturally is somewhere about 1808. Martin Burney, I should first say, was the son of Admiral Burney, who sailed with Cook, and the nephew of Madame D'Arblay. He was about Lamb's age, but Lamb was much older in every way, and in fact a deal of Martin had probably never grown up. He was a gentle creature with a kind of doglike affection for his friends, no sense of practical life whatever, and liable to very foolish impulses. The Lambs were very fond of him. He outlived both, and wept at Mary Lamb's funeral with a lack of restraint which Crabb Robinson found offensive.

'Here is the first letter:

'MY DEAR MARTIN,

'I send this by our good friend Ayrton to tell you that the time for self-reproach and hiding has past. As to what you have done, I have only an impaired inkling; but I know your nature and what it would never do, and I say in all gravity and love, absent thee from felicity no longer. You have had your share; it is not well to indulge oneself too far in abnegation. Remember moreover that you are not alone: you are part of a family. The right to chastise ourselves is no doubt one that human beings will cherish as long as most; but a time comes when the question must be put, Are we not chastening the innocent too? You must search your heart with that inquiry at once, Martin, and when you have supplied the only answer, you must hasten back to Little James Street to comfort your poor mother and restore in the Admiral—who, I am in a position to inform you, is not so angry as he pretends, having himself once been young—a desire for a rubber. All is not lost because one has been foolish.

'Yours most truly,
'C. LAMB

'In 1818, Lamb, thinking his literary career over (before it had really begun), collected his *Works* in two volumes, and they were dedicated to Martin Burney in a sonnet, ending with the beautiful lines:

'In all thy threading of this worldly maze
(And I have watched thee almost from a child),
Free from self-seeking, envy, low design,
I have not found a whiter soul than thine.

'Here is the very letter that accompanied the dedicatory sonnet:

'20 GREAT RUSSELL STREET
'*April 8th*, 1818

'DEAR LAD, as I shall always call you no matter how grey you become or how senile you talk, this is the sonnet which I wish to inscribe on a fly leaf of my WORKS—WORKS! do you hear? —so that they may have at any rate one page of which I shall never feel ashamed. For the rest, I alternate between misgiving and a feeling that a few things there may be neatly said, but whether I would like to burn them or write them all over again, I am undecided. Am I clear?

'My WORKS—henceforward *your* WORKS by

virtue of this fourteener—are going to be in two plump little volumes. Have you ever had twins before? I am an old hand at it, for the Poetry for Children and the Tales from Shakespeare were gemini too.

'Thine,

'C. L.

'In 1821 the Admiral published his *Essay on the Game of Whist*, and Lamb wrote to congratulate him on it. There is no date:

'MY DEAR ADMIRAL,

'I have now perused your treatise with pleasure and edification. Since you would not give me one, and since I buy no new books, I have had to borrow Martin's copy, and I adjure you when next you see him to tell him from me that he must extract another from the paternal store, for never will I part with *mine*, as I now call it.

'That is the only true subject for the Essayist's pen—Whist, the only game in which intellect and recreation equally participate. You make me ashamed of the frivolous wayward saunterings of my *London* pen, concerned as it is with such trifles as the South Sea House, New Year's Eve, Christ's Hospital, and so forth. Looking back upon my recent bewildering activities—to think of any sane man recommencing author at my age, after the publication of his *Works* too!—I charge myself with writing real sense only in that paper wherein Sarah Battle unbosoms on the Great

Topic, your Topic and—henceforward—mine.
'Yours till the last Trump, and, as a Christian,
I trust, after,

'C. L.

'And here', Mr. Ingleside added, 'is a note,
in the doctor's hand, to the effect that Lamb
kept his word about not returning Martin's
copy, for it was sold after his death with other
volumes from his library.

'The next letter is dated November 18, 1821,
the day after the Admiral's death:

'MY DEAR MARTIN,
    'The sad news was brought by Ayrton.
We had heard there was no hope; but the shock
of the death of an old friend cannot to any appre-
ciable extent be softened by foreknowledge. He
was and he is not: that is the immitigable fact.
A time has come when it seems that none of my
friends are safe; and you would be wise to avoid
me. Don't be seen with me. Run when I appear.
There's Jem White gone; and then, only a month
ago, my brother; and now your father. We shall
soon be alone, Martin. Give your mother our
love. I say "our" but I have not told Mary yet.
Her recovery is so recent I hesitate to do so; and
this will explain my absence from the funeral.
As to that other matter, I am doing what I can
and shall see J. R. shortly.
    'May God bless us all.

'C. L.

'The phrase "that other matter",' Mr. Ingleside added, 'is said in the pencil note to refer to some difficulty that Martin Burney had been having with his employer, John Rickman, Clerk Assistant at the Table of the House of Commons, and Lamb's friend.

'The two next are more frivolous:

'DEAR MARTIN [the date is 7 November, 1823, Colebrooke Cottage, Islington]
'Dear Martin, we count on you for Sunday. Leg of lamb at three precisely. If you fail us you will miss the sight of the season—G. D.'s diluvian shoes, still drying in the garden from his immersion. He forbade us to set them near the fire, as heat cracketh them—as though aught could crack further such cracks as Time has been making these twenty years. But come and see them. You cannot miss them: they hang on the line.
'Thine,
'C. L.

'G. D. is of course George Dyer, who, being nearly blind, had walked into the New River in front of Lamb's house a few days before. The next is a year later:

'DEAR MARTIN,
'You offered once to let us use your subscription at Cawthorn's Library when you were circuiting up and down in the land seeking whom you might defend. Mary is sadly hipped at this

moment, and was never so destitute of such light fictions as C. disburses. Will you authorise him to send her a bundle no matter how foolish? Hazlitt——

'The rest is torn away,' said Mr. Ingleside. 'What a loss!

'We come now to a letter to Mrs. Burney, referring to the essay "The Wedding" to be found in the second volume of *Elia*:

'COLEBROOKE COTTAGE
'*May 24th*, 1825

'MY DEAR MRS. BURNEY,
'In the forthcoming *London* look out for some recollections of happier days for all of us —although I must not talk like that lest the Powers hear me and punish me for ingratitude, since I am now free and well. Mary has not been ill for so long that I tremble when I count the months. Recollection then of happier days, let me say, for you, for I have been sending my memory back to Sarah's wedding and my foolishness with the Admiral afterwards. You will not be offended, I know. I am a sad autobiographer, and none of my friends are safe when the *London* clamours, and when, having nothing but time, as now, I have none. I must try to get to Little James Street soon and once more shake you by the hand.
'Your sincere friend,
'CHARLES LAMB

'Mary sends her love and wishes that the rubbers were not all over. So do I. But then I wish so many things.

'The next letter was written only a day after. To Martin. It explains itself:

'COLEBROOKE COTTAGE
'*May 25th*, 1825

'DEAR MARTIN,
'News has just come that my brother John's widow has joined him in that place where there is neither marriage nor giving in marriage, but where I presume husbands and wives do not have to be reintroduced when they meet. I must, since I am not only her brother-in-law but executor, attend the funeral. Will you come to Colebrooke on Sunday and explicate the last will and testament to my jaded apprehensions? I saw it once and I recollect with alarm how it bristled with the terms of your Mystery, and with what advantage a pepper-pot could be filled with commas and periods and sprinkled over it. There is so little money for the relict's daughter that I wish to get my legal advice free as the air we breathe, which, so far as I have been able to observe during a pilgrimage of almost exactly fifty years, is the only gratuitous commodity that exists.
'Thine,
'C. L.

'A note', said Mr. Ingleside, 'remarks that Lamb was taken ill almost directly after this letter and remained ill for some time, while his sister failed again too. The last is not dated at all:

'DEAR MARTIN,
      'A barrel of oysters has fallen upon us from the blue; we know not at whose bidding, but each has a guess. I like to stand aside and watch my friends engage in combats of generosity, and I care not who is the winner so they fight gamely and exchange shrewd blows. Oysters will be on the table at nine to-morrow with concomitant porter. We shall be disappointed if you eat none of them.'

'A phrase or two of that letter, or something very like it, is repeated in Lamb's "Thoughts on Presents of Game",' said Dr. Staminer. 'Perhaps we may date it somewhere at the same time—in 1830. But it doesn't matter.'

1910

P.S.—Since this was written—in fact, only the other day—an authentic letter from Lamb to Martin Burney has come to light. It is dated March 19, 1829, and contains an album poem.

1933

THE LAST DAYS

WHEN, in April or May 1833, Charles Lamb moved into 'Oak Cottage', Edmonton, he was fifty-eight and in a very unhappy, disenchanted way. His sister had preceded him there from Enfield to be in the care of the tenants, Mr. and Mrs. Walden, who were mental nurses: it was indeed a private asylum. With Lamb went Emma Isola, his adopted daughter and his only companion on his walks, but it was no place for her, and she seems to have lodged elsewhere; also she had just become engaged to Edward Moxon, the publisher, so that her days with Lamb were in any case numbered.

What kind of life Lamb led alone, we can only sadly conjecture. As I walked through this melancholy house, the sense of tragedy deepened with every step. It has hardly been touched since Lamb's time—the same wainscotting, the same windows, although the Hogarth prints are no longer there and the books, of course, have gone; but you may reconstruct the past only too vividly. It is the darkest house I ever saw, wedged between two larger ones, with evergreens to obscure the front, and fruit trees to obscure the back; and you may picture Lamb in his gloomy sitting-room considering what to do next; imagine him standing by the front gate, watching the street, or starting on his lonely trampings, with too many hostelries *en route*. Then back again, with the half hope that a miracle had happened in the interval and his sister was suddenly herself again; only to find it a fallacy and another long solitary evening before him.

We have a glimpse of the Lambs at Edmonton in the reminiscences of an old inhabitant contributed to the *Globe* in 1875:

'Nearly opposite the cottage,' he says, 'and the first object on which Lamb's eye would rest as he pushed at the high iron gate that shut in his strip of garden, stands a charity school for girls. . . . The mistress, still living in a hale old age, was often drawn to the window by Lamb's cheery voice as he issued from Mr. Walden's, chatting loudly with anyone he used to meet. He would accost passers-by, she says, and walk with them down the street. Otherwise he was not noticeable, except as a spare, middle-sized man, in panta-loons. Mary Lamb would sometimes, but not often, be seen in the street alone. The reputation of insanity attaches, in the schoolmistress's mind, to the brother as well as the sister.'

The charity school now has a new façade, but the old charming figure of a typical scholar remains in a niche.

In May 1834 Mary was recovering, as Lamb tells Manning:

> We play Picquet, and it is like the old times a while, then goes off. I walk nine or ten miles a day, always up the road, dear London-wards.

On June 7th she was well enough to play a rubber of whist with her brother and Crabb Robinson. On June 19th both Charles and Mary breakfasted with the same friend to meet N. P. Willis, the American writer, who has left a lively account of the occasion. He describes Lamb as having

> 'his head set on his shoulders with a thoughtful, forward bent, his hair just sprinkled with grey, a beautiful deep-set eye, aquiline nose, and a very indescribable mouth. Whether it expressed most humour or feeling, good-nature or a kind of whimsical peevishness, or twenty other things which passed over it by turns, I cannot in the least be certain.' Miss Lamb was 'a small, bent figure, evidently a victim to ill-health, and hears with difficulty. . . . I had set a large armchair for Miss Lamb. "Don't take it, Mary," said Lamb, pulling it away from her very gravely, "it looks as if you were going to have a tooth drawn."

'Lamb', Willis continues, 'ate nothing, and complained in a querulous tone of the veal-pie. There was a kind of potted fish (of which I forget the name at this moment) which he had expected our friend would procure for him. He inquired whether there was not a morsel left perhaps in the bottom of the last pot. Mr. R. was not sure. "Send and see," said Lamb, "and if the pot has been cleaned bring me the cover. I think the sight of it would do me good." The cover was brought, upon which there was a picture of the fish. Lamb kissed it with a reproachful look at his friend, and then left the table. . . .'

That was June, and we can see that Lamb was in a poor state of nerves and spirits. On July 25th came the stunning blow: Coleridge died, and with him Lamb began to die, too; but there were still five months. . . .

The end came through a fall on his way towards the Bell on December 22nd; erysipelas set in, and he died on the 27th, and was buried in Edmonton churchyard six days later. In 1847, when his sister died, the grave was opened and she was laid there, too.

As to this grave, which the sexton tells me is constantly visited, it has a plain headstone with the verses on it by H. F. Cary, father of the Cary who painted the picture of Charles and Mary Lamb which is now in the National Portrait Gallery. In 1868, I find, there was an effort to obtain money for a bust to be placed there. At the beginning of the edition of *The Complete Correspondence and Works by Charles Lamb with an Essay on his Life and Genius by George Augustus Sala*, which Moxon & Co. projected but which never proceeded beyond the first volume, is an appeal for funds for a memorial in Edmonton churchyard 'to replace the tasteless headstone that is there now', the new tomb and bust to be executed by Thomas Woolner, Esq. Subscriptions were to be sent to Mr. Moxon; but subscriptions never came.

At the moment Lamb is without any right memorial. There is the fountain in the Temple garden; there are tablets on three of the houses where he lived: 2 Crown Office Row, where he was born; Colebrooke Cottage, Islington; and "Lamb Cottage" at Edmonton, where his noble spirit took flight; and there is a relief at Christ's Hospital. Should not something more be done? I personally should like to see a seated statue of him, in the manner of Boehm's Carlyle, just inside the railings facing 2 Crown Office Row: an ideal situation.

1925–33

THE EMBARRASSED ELIMINATORS

WE were talking about Lamb.

Some one suddenly asked: 'Supposing that by an incredible Soviet decree all his essays except one were to be destroyed, which one would you keep?'

This kind of question is always interesting, no matter to what author's work or to what picture gallery it is applied. But for the best resulting literary talk it must be applied to Shakespeare, to Dickens, or to Elia.

'Why, of course,' at once said H., whose pleasant habit it is to rush in with a final opinion on everything at a moment's notice, with no shame whatever in changing it immediately afterwards, 'there's no doubt about it at all—Mrs. Battle. Absolutely impossible to give up Mrs. Battle. Or, wait a minute, I'd forgotten Bo-Bo,—"The Dissertation on Roast Pig," you know. Either Mrs. Battle or that.'

The man who had propounded the question laughed. 'I saw that second string coming,' he said. 'That's what every one wants: one *or* another. But the whole point of the thing is that one essay and one only is to remain: everything else goes by the board. Now? Let's leave H. to wrestle it out with himself. What do *you* say, James?'

'It's too difficult,' said James. 'I was going to say "The Old Actors" until I remembered several others. But I'm not sure that that is not my choice. It stands alone in literature: it is Lamb inimitable. His literary descendants have done their best and worst with most of his methods, but here, where knowledge of the world, knowledge of the stage, love of mankind, gusto, humour, style and imaginative understanding unite, the mimics are left behind. Miles. Yes, I vote for "The Old Actors".'

'But, my dear James,' said L., 'think a moment. Remember James Elia in "My Relations"; remember Cousin Bridget in "Mackery End". You are prepared deliberately to have these for ever blotted out of your consciousness? Because, as I understand it, that is what the question means: utter elimination.'

James groaned. 'It's too serious,' he said. 'It's not really to be thought of. It reminds me of terrible nights at school when I lay awake trying to understand eternity—complete negation—until I turned giddy with the immensity of dark nothingness.'

Our host laughed. 'You were very positive just now,' he said. 'But have you forgotten a wistful little trifle called "Old China"?'

'Or, more on your own lines,' said W., 'nearer your actors and acting, the "South-Sea House" or the "Old Benchers"? I will grant you the perfection—there is no other word—of the full-lengths of Dicky Suett and Bannister and Bensley's Malvolio. There is nothing like it—you are quite right. Not even Hazlitt comes near it. One can see oneself with a great effort doing something passably Hazlittian in dramatic criticism, if one were put to it; but Lamb, Lamb reconstructs life and dignifies and enriches it as he does so. That essay in my opinion is the justification of footlights, grease-paint, and all the tawdry business. And yet'—W.'s face glowed with his eloquence, as it always does sooner or later every evening—'and yet if I were restricted to one *Elia* essay—dreadful thought!—it would not be "The Old Actors" that I should choose, but—I can't help it— "Captain Jackson". I know there are far more beautiful things in Elia; deeper, sweeter, rarer. But the Captain and I are such old friends that it comes to this, I couldn't do without him.'

'Of course,' cried H., 'I had forgotten. You

remind me of something I simply must keep—
the Elliston.' He snatched the *Essays* from
our host's hands and read the following passage,
while we all laughed—a double laughter—
overtly with him, and covertly at him, for if
there is one man living who might be the hero
to-day of a similar story it is H. himself, who
has a capriciousness, an impulsiveness, a forget-
fulness, and a grandiosity that are Ellistonian
or nothing.

Those who knew Elliston [he read] will know
the manner in which he pronounced the latter
sentence of the few words I am about to
record. One proud day to me he took his roast
mutton with us in the Temple, to which I had
superadded a haddock. After a rather plentiful
partaking of the meagre banquet, not unrefreshed
with the humbler sorts of liquors, I made a sort
of apology for the humility of the fare, observing
that for my own part I never ate but of one dish
at dinner. 'I too never eat but one thing at
dinner,'—was his reply—then after a pause—
'reckoning fish as nothing.' The manner was all.
It was as if by one peremptory sentence he had
decreed the annihilation of all the savoury
esculents which the pleasant and nutritious-food-
giving Ocean pours forth upon poor humans
from her watery bosom. This was greatness,
tempered with considerate tenderness to the
feelings of his scanty but welcoming entertainer.

'Well,' said our host, reclaiming the book, 'my vote if I had one would be for "Mackery End in Hertfordshire"; and I make the declaration quite calmly, knowing that we are all safe to retain what we will. James will of course disagree with the choice; but then you see I am a sentimentalist, and when Lamb writes about his sister and his childhood I am lost. And "Mackery End" delights me in two ways, for it not only has the wonderful picture of Bridget Elia in it, but we see Lamb also on one of his rapturous walks in his own county. I never see a field of wheat without recalling his phrase of Hertfordshire as "that fine corn country".'

'All very well,' said James, 'but if you talk like this how are you going to let "Dream Children" go?'

'Ah, yes,' sighed our host, ' "Dream Children"—of course! How could I let that go? No, it's too difficult.'

'What about this?' said the grave incisive voice of K., who had not yet spoken, and he began to read:

> In proportion as the years both lessen and shorten, I set more count upon their periods, and would fain lay my ineffectual finger upon the spoke of the great wheel. I am not content to pass

away 'like a weaver's shuttle'. Those metaphors
solace me not, nor sweeten the unpalatable draught
of mortality. I care not to be carried with the tide,
that smoothly bears human life to eternity; and
reluct at the inevitable course of destiny. I am
in love with this green earth; the face of town
and country; the unspeakable rural solitudes,
and the sweet security of streets.

'Who is going to forswear that passage?'
K. asked sternly, fixing his eyes on us as if we
were one and all guilty of damnable heresy.

We all sighed.

K. searched the book again, and again began
to read:

In sober verity I will confess a truth to thee,
reader. I love a Fool—as naturally as if I were
of kith and kin to him. When a child, with child-
like apprehensions, that dived not below the
surface of the matter, I read those Parables—
not guessing at the involved wisdom—I had more
yearnings towards that simple architect, that
built his house upon the sand, than I entertained
for his more cautious neighbour: I grudged at
the hard censure pronounced upon the quiet
soul that kept his talent; and—prizing their
simplicity beyond the more provident, and, to
my apprehension, somewhat unfeminine wariness
of their competitors—I felt a kindliness, that
almost amounted to a *tendre*, for those five thought-
less virgins.

'Who is going to turn his back for ever on that passage? No,' K. went on, 'it won't do. It is not possible to name one essay and one only. But I have an amendment to propose. Instead of being permitted to retain only one essay, why should we not be allowed a series of passages equal in length to the longest essay —say "The Old Actors"? Then we should not be quite so hopeless. That, for example, would enable one to keep the page on Bensley's Malvolio, the description of Bridget Elia, a portion of the "Mrs. Battle", Ralph Bigod, a portion of "Captain Jackson", the passages I have read, and—what I personally should insist upon including, earlier almost than any-thing—the Fallacies on Rising with the Lark and Retiring with the Lamb.'

'Well,' said the suggester of the original problem, 'it's a compromise and therefore no fun. But you may play with it if you like. The sweepingness of the first question was of course its merit. James is the only one of you with the courage really to make a choice.'

'Oh, no,' said our host. 'I chose one and one only instantly—"Old China".'

'Nonsense!' said James; 'you chose "Mac-kery End".'

'There you are,' said K. 'That shows.'

'Well, I refuse to be deprived of "Old China" anyway,' said our host, 'even if I named "Mackery End". How could one live without "Old China"? Our discussion reminds me', he added, 'of a very pretty poem—a kind of poem that is no longer written. It is by an American who came nearer Lamb in humour and "the tact of humanity" than perhaps any writer—the Autocrat. Let me read it to you.'

He reached for a volume and read as follows:

> Oh for one hour of youthful joy!
> Give back my twentieth spring!
> I'd rather laugh, a bright-haired boy,
> That reign, a grey-beard king.
>
> Off with the spoils of wrinkled age!
> Away with Learning's crown!
> Tear out Life's Wisdom-written page,
> And dash its trophies down!
>
> One moment let my life-blood stream
> From boyhood's fount of flame!
> Give me one giddy, reeling dream
> Of life all love and fame!
>
> .   .   .   .   .
>
> My listening angel heard the prayer,
> And, calmly smiling, said,
> 'If I but touch thy silvered hair
> Thy hasty wish hath sped.

138

'But is there nothing in thy track,
    To bid thee fondly stay,
While the swift seasons hurry back
    To find the wished-for day?'

'Ah, truest soul of womankind!
    Without thee what were life
One bliss I cannot leave behind:
    I'll take—my—precious—wife!'

The angel took a sapphire pen
    And wrote in rainbow dew,
The man would be a boy again,
    And be a husband too!

'And is there nothing yet unsaid,
    Before the change appears?
Remember, all their gifts have fled
    With those dissolving years.'

'Why, yes;' for memory would recall
    My fond paternal joys;
'I could not bear to leave them all—
    I'll take—my—girl—and—boys.'

The smiling angel dropped his pen—
    'Why this will never do;
The man would be a boy again,
    And be a father too!'

   .   .   .   .   .

And so I laughed—my laughter woke
    The household with its noise—
And wrote my dream, when morning broke
    To please the grey-haired boys.

'We', said our host, as he closed the book and laid it aside, 'are like that: we would surrender most of Elia and have him whole too.'

'Yes,' said W. 'Exactly. We want them all and we value them the more as we grow older and they grow truer and better. For that is Lamb's way. He sat down—often in his employers' time—to amuse the readers of a new magazine and earn a few of those extra guineas which made it possible to write "Old China", and behold he was shedding radiance on almost every fact of life, no matter how spiritually recondite or remote from his own practical experience. No one can rise from Elia without being deepened and enriched; and no one having read Elia can ever say either off-hand or after a year's thought which one essay he would retain to the loss of all the others.'

B. hitherto had been a silent listener. Here he spoke, and, as so often, said the final thing. 'Yes,' he said, 'it is vain (but good sport) to take any one of the essays and argue that it is the best. Just as the best thing in a garden is not any particular flower but the scent of all the flowers that are there, so the best of Lamb is not any single essay but the fragrance of them all. It is for this that those paths have been trodden by so much good company.

'Yes,' he added meditatively. ' "The scent of Elia's garden"! That is the best essay, if you like, and "Charles (and Mary) Lamb" its title.'

1911